TORONTO MAPLE LEAFS

IMAGES OF GLORY

JAMES DUPLACEY
JOSEPH ROMAIN

McGraw-Hill Ryerson
Toronto Montreal

Toronto Maple Leafs: Images of Glory

First published in 1990 by
McGraw-Hill Ryerson Limited
330 Progress Avenue
Scarborough, Ontario
M1P 2Z5

The photographs and other artifacts in the Hockey Hall of Fame come to the museum as parts of personal or private collections. It has therefore not always been possible to identify originating photographers. The authors and the Hockey Hall of Fame welcome any additional information on the photographs in this book.

Editor: Andrea Gallagher Ellis

Design and Production: Lynda Powell

Colour Separations and Typesetting: Compeer Typographic Services

ISBN 0-07-551063-4

1 2 3 4 5 6 7 8 9 0 D 9 8 7 6 5 4 3 2 1 0

Printed and bound in Canada by John Deyell Company

Canadian Cataloguing in Publication Data

Duplacey, James
Toronto Maple Leafs: Images of Glory

ISBN 0-07-551063-4

1. Toronto Maple Leafs (Hockey team) — Pictorial works.
2. Toronto Maple Leafs (Hockey team) — History.
I. Romain, Joseph. II. Title

GV848.T6D8 1990 796.962'64'09713541 C90-095565-1

Overleaf
Stanley Cup Champions, 1967. HHF Archival Collection

Contents

"This shows the 1967 Stanley Cup team congratulating Bobby Pulford who scored in overtime. We were not favoured to win that particular year. Montreal, having won the two previous years, was looking forward to 1967 because of Expo. We went ahead and beat them, and it was quite an upset — one of the biggest in hockey history." — Frank Mahovlich

Frank Prazak Collection, HHF

Preface

Images of Glory is a pictorial celebration of the Toronto Maple Leafs that brings together some of the best Leaf photographs of recent decades with rare old archival material to give a comprehensive picture of professional hockey in Toronto over the last hundred years.

We have included more than 250 photographs from the Hockey Hall of Fame and Museum (HHF), Bruce Bennett Studios, Graphic Artists, and the Toronto Telegram Collection at York University. The pictures take the reader from the earliest formation of a professional Toronto franchise in

"There's Ace Bailey, the first Leaf ever to win a scoring championship. Bailey, Blair, and Cotton made a very exciting line to watch." — Tommy Gaston

Imperial Oil Turofsky Collection, HHF

Bob Pulford takes a pass from Jimmy Pappin to end 28 minutes of overtime and give the Leafs a 3–2 win in game three of the 1967 Stanley Cup finals.

Frank Prazak Collection, HHF

the National Hockey Association and its evolution to the Toronto Maple Leafs, through the great years of the 1940s and the 1960s, to the struggles of the 1980s.

The text provides sufficient detail to make even the most casual fan an expert where historical trivia is concerned, such as who was the first Leaf to score a goal, and which Leaf scored a pure hat trick in overtime. In many instances we asked the players themselves to comment on the photographs; among those whose comments were solicited are Ace Bailey, Bob Davidson, Teeder Kennedy, Frank Mahovlich, Red Kelly, Ron Ellis, Lanny McDonald, Brad Marsh, and Rob Ramage.

We have also tried to present a fan's perspective, to hear the voices of those paying customers who have kept Maple Leaf Gardens filled to near capacity for Leaf games since it was built 60 years ago. Tom Gaston has been a Leaf season-ticket holder for 50 years and is a dedicated volunteer at the Hockey Hall of Fame. Esther Richards, the executive secretary at the Hockey Hall of Fame, used to collect Beehive hockey cards of the Leafs and sit in the dark with her little brother on Saturday nights, long after the rest of the family had gone to bed, listening to Foster Hewitt's radio play-by-play, when Syl Apps, Turk Broda, and Teeder Kennedy were the reigning kings of the ice. Jack Felstead, whose family includes four generations of Leaf fans, is the official historian for the Toronto Maple Leafs. Their comments have enriched our text.

Images of Glory is an informal look at the history of the team, with profiles of some of the outstanding players who embody the spirit of the Toronto Maple Leafs. It is a book about the heart and drive of the Leafs, to many the best-loved team in the history of Canadian sport.

Hockey in the olden days was played by invincible men whose exploits only become more glorious with the passage of time. Powerful rightwinger Charlie Conacher, "The Big Bomber," was a four-time NHL goal-scoring champion and played on five all-star teams.

Tom Gaston Collection, HHF

Acknowledgements

Many individuals, publications, and events have helped to inspire, research, and expedite this project. Through the encouragement of Glen Ellis at McGraw-Hill Ryerson, they all conspired to complete *Images of Glory*, and, though most of them will remain anonymous, there are a few who must be identified.

Tom Gaston, our "blue and white guru," was a tireless and inspirational cheerleader and a fount of trivia. We are grateful to Jack Felstead, who compiled all the statistics, and to Esther Richards for her enthusiasm and her keen insight. Dan Diamond of Dan Diamond and Associates, as ever, was a brick.

Our thanks go also to Ralph Dinger, proprietor of The Ice Age, who met and interviewed the many Toronto Maple Leafs whose comments are a valuable contribution to this book. Ace Bailey, Frank Mahovlich, Ron Ellis, Red Kelly, Bob Davidson, Teeder Kennedy, Brad Marsh, Rob Ramage, and Lanny McDonald all continue to contribute to the glory of the team through their memories and insights. For this, we humbly thank them.

Among the publications we consulted during the course of our research are Charles Coleman's *The Trail of the Stanley Cup;* Stan and Shirley Fischler's *Encyclopedia of Hockey;* Foster Hewitt's *Hockey Night in Canada;* the Hockey Hall of Fame and Museum's *Hockey News Index;* William Houston's *Inside Maple Leaf Gardens: The Rise and Fall of the Toronto Maple Leafs;* Punch Imlach's *Heaven and Hell in the NHL* and *Hockey Is a Battle;* Stan Obodiac's *Red Kelly* and *The Leafs: The First Fifty Years;* Frank Selke's (with Gordon Green) *Behind the Cheering;* Conn Smythe's (with Scott Young) *If You Can't Beat 'em in the Alley;* and Scott Young's *The Leafs I Knew.*

Finally, this book is a celebration in pictures of the Toronto Maple Leafs, and so, to all those photographers who have chronicled the Leafs over the years and whose work is represented here, thank you.

Frank Mahovlich
Imperial Oil Turofsky Collection, HHF

To Tommy Gaston, a great friend, and perhaps the biggest Leaf fan of them all

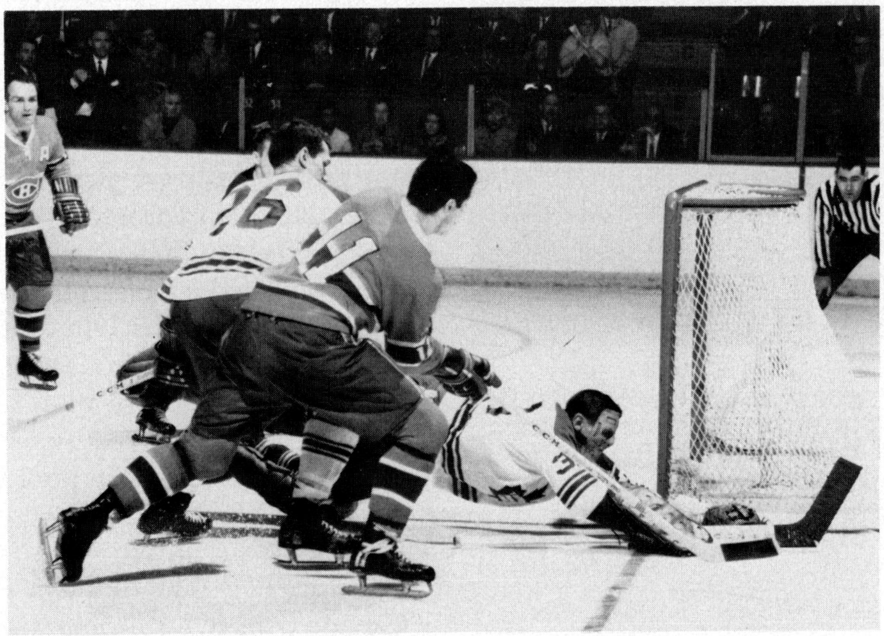

Terry Sawchuk dives to keep a loose puck out of the grasp of Montreal Canadiens' forward Claude Larose during the 1967 Stanley Cup finals. Allan Stanley stands poised to give Sawchuk a helping hand as Henri Richard awaits a possible centring pass. Veterans Stanley and Sawchuk were instrumental in helping the underdog Leafs to a Centennial year Cup win.

Frank Prazak Collection, HHF

Images of Glory

The legendary Conn Smythe proposed several laughable business deals, but he took big gambles — and laughed all the way to the bank. Among his many accomplishments are the founding of the Toronto Maple Leafs and the construction of Maple Leaf Gardens. He was also a moving force in the development of the Hockey Hall of Fame in Toronto.

Imperial Oil Turofsky Collection, HHF

Officially, the Toronto Maple Leaf Hockey Club came into being on February 14, 1927. When Toronto's National Hockey League franchise, the St. Patricks, went up for sale, Conn Smythe, determined to keep the team in Toronto, formed a consortium and bought the club, renaming it the Toronto Maple Leafs. But the history of the club stretches back further than its name — to the beginnings of hockey in Toronto.

The cities of Halifax, Kingston, Montreal, and Windsor (Nova Scotia) have all claimed at one time or another to be the birthplace of ice hockey. Stick and ball games were played in all these places and undoubtedly in Toronto as well. Toronto, however, makes no claim to have invented the game — only to have played it well from the time of its introduction at the end of the 19th century.

We first find a Toronto team in competition at the Montreal Ice Carnival in 1884 in the first known organized series played under written rules. Hockey quickly grew in popularity and spread across the country. There were countless small leagues of four or five teams radiating out from the Ottawa Valley. The Amateur Hockey Association of Canada (AHAC) was organized in 1886 and the Ontario Hockey Association (OHA) in 1890. Governor General Lord Stanley donated the Stanley Cup in 1893, to be presented to Canada's championship amateur hockey team; there were as yet no professional teams.

At the end of the 1893 season the Ottawa City Club and Toronto's Osgoode Hall team had the two highest standings in the OHA and were ordered by the trustees of the Stanley Cup to play for the prize. The Ottawa club refused the challenge, maintaining that their defeat of the Osgoode Hall team a few weeks earlier was proof enough that they were the

The 1904 Marlborough Hockey Club was the second Toronto-based team to challenge for the Stanley Cup. The first was the Toronto Wellingtons of 1902, of whom no photographs have surfaced. This photo of the 1905 Marlies includes three of the defeated warriors (Charlton, Winchester, and Birmingham) who fell to the powerful Ottawa City Club in 1904.
HHF Archival Collection

better team. At this point the trustees went to the AHAC and the Cup was awarded to the champions of that league, the Montreal Amateur Athletic Association. So, Toronto never really had a chance to compete for the first Stanley Cup. Had the playoff with Ottawa been held, it is arguable that the Toronto squad might have gone down as the first winners of hockey's most enduring symbol and the oldest trophy for professional athletes in North America.

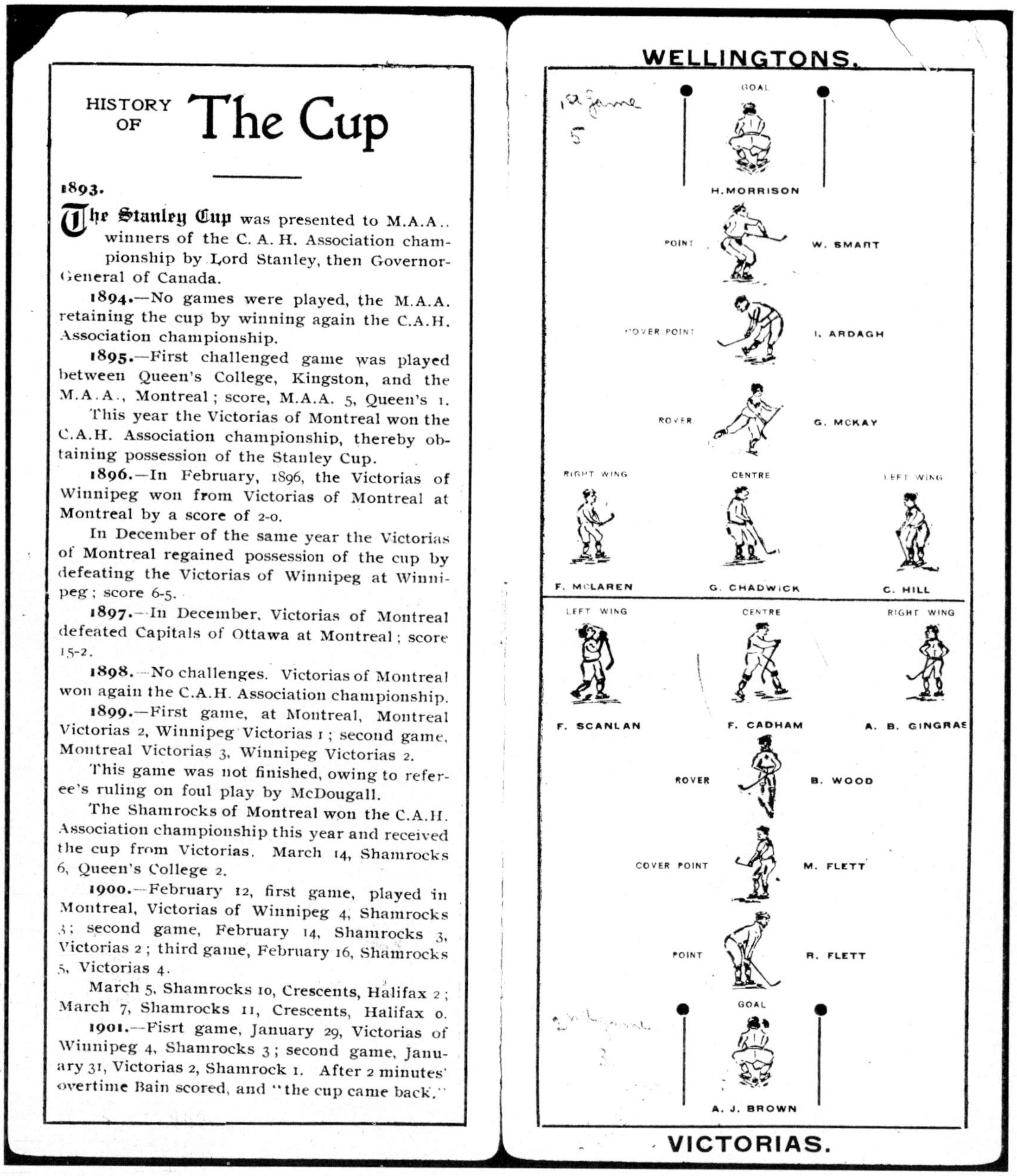

HISTORY OF **The Cup**

1893.

The Stanley Cup was presented to M.A.A., winners of the C. A. H. Association championship by Lord Stanley, then Governor-General of Canada.

1894.—No games were played, the M.A.A. retaining the cup by winning again the C.A.H. Association championship.

1895.—First challenged game was played between Queen's College, Kingston, and the M.A.A., Montreal; score, M.A.A. 5, Queen's 1.

This year the Victorias of Montreal won the C.A.H. Association championship, thereby obtaining possession of the Stanley Cup.

1896.—In February, 1896, the Victorias of Winnipeg won from Victorias of Montreal at Montreal by a score of 2-0.

In December of the same year the Victorias of Montreal regained possession of the cup by defeating the Victorias of Winnipeg at Winnipeg; score 6-5.

1897.—In December, Victorias of Montreal defeated Capitals of Ottawa at Montreal; score 15-2.

1898.—No challenges. Victorias of Montreal won again the C.A.H. Association championship.

1899.—First game, at Montreal, Montreal Victorias 2, Winnipeg Victorias 1; second game, Montreal Victorias 3, Winnipeg Victorias 2.

This game was not finished, owing to referee's ruling on foul play by McDougall.

The Shamrocks of Montreal won the C.A.H. Association championship this year and received the cup from Victorias. March 14, Shamrocks 6, Queen's College 2.

1900.—February 12, first game, played in Montreal, Victorias of Winnipeg 4, Shamrocks 3; second game, February 14, Shamrocks 3, Victorias 2; third game, February 16, Shamrocks 5, Victorias 4.

March 5, Shamrocks 10, Crescents, Halifax 2; March 7, Shamrocks 11, Crescents, Halifax 0.

1901.—Fisrt game, January 29, Victorias of Winnipeg 4, Shamrocks 3; second game, January 31, Victorias 2, Shamrock 1. After 2 minutes' overtime Bain scored, and "the cup came back."

This early "hockey program" gives a brief history of the Stanley Cup and lists the positions as well as the players in the 1902 Cup final.
HHF Archival Collection

It was not until 1902 that a Toronto team, the Wellingtons, skated out onto Stanley Cup ice. Their opponents, the Winnipeg Victorias, were the Cup holders at the time and handed the Wellingtons two losses, both with a score of 5–3. For decades the records of this series were lost to the light of day, but in more recent years historians have uncovered the stories of this and several other Stanley Cup challenges.

In 1904 the Toronto Marlboroughs, champions of the OHA, challenged the mighty Ottawa Silver Seven for the Cup. The series ran to just two games, the Marlies returning to Toronto empty handed after suffering losses of 6–3 and 11–2.

Although professional hockey had made its debut in the United States in 1902, it was still largely frowned upon in Canada. Players in centres like Toronto and Montreal were more than likely to be sporting young gentlemen from the universities who played for honour and the love of sport. Players were not generally paid, although this practice was not always honoured in the observance. Many of the best players were in fact compensated for their services, especially in the bush leagues, but the idea of an outright professional league was still sniffed at in many quarters.

The newly prosperous lumber and mineral barons of the early 1900s — the Bickells, the O'Briens, and the Patricks, for instance — had no such traditional ethical qualms. Bush leagues flourished in the mining and logging centres across the country, and it soon became apparent that a hockey team —

The Allan Cup, first donated by Sir Montagu Allan in 1909, remains a symbol of amateur hockey excellence.
HHF Archival Collection

The great Edouard "Newsy" Lalonde is not remembered for his time with the Toronto Trolley Leaguers, but in 1908 and 1909 he was the star forward for an oft-forgotten Cup challenger, the Torontos of the OPHL. Lalonde went on to become a founding member of the Montreal Canadiens of the NHA and NHL, where he played 10 seasons. He was elected to the Hockey Hall to Fame in 1950.
HHF Archival Collection

better still a league — could be a paying proposition.

Among the first overtly professional teams in Canada were the Torontos of the Ontario Professional Hockey League (OPHL). Formed in 1908, the OPHL was known as the Trolley League, because all the competing towns and cities, including Guelph, Berlin (Kitchener), St. Catherines, Brantford, and Toronto, were connected by electric rail lines. As champions of the OPHL for 1908, the Torontos challenged the current national champions, the Montreal Wanderers of the Eastern Canada Hockey Association (ECHA), for possession of the Stanley Cup. It was a single-game challenge in which Toronto standouts Newsy Lalonde, Bruce Ridpath, and Rowley Young found the mark, but they came up short, losing 6–4 to the Wanderers.

By 1908 there were several professional leagues based in eastern Canada, and by 1910 professional hockey had virtually taken over the Stanley Cup competition. It was at this point, therefore, that William Northey, president of the Montreal AAA, prevailed upon Sir H. Montagu Allan, a prominent Montreal banker, shipowner, and sportsman, to donate a challenge trophy, the Allan Cup, to honour senior amateur hockey in Canada.

J. Ambrose O'Brien, a silver-mining magnate from Renfrew, Ontario, established the National Hockey Association (NHA) in 1909. At the time, the dominant Eastern Canada Hockey Association had just dissolved itself and regrouped under the name of the Canadian Hockey Association (CHA) in a strategic attempt to freeze out the troublesome Montreal Wanderers. O'Brien applied to the CHA for a franchise in Renfrew, but CHA officials felt that Renfrew was too small, so O'Brien turned around and formed his own league in collaboration with the Wanderers' owners. O'Brien's National Hockey Association (NHA), the immediate predecessor of today's National Hockey League (NHL), officially began play on January 10, 1910. The NHA had five teams: Renfrew, Cobalt, Haileybury, the Montreal Wanderers, and a new team, Les Canadiens of Montreal.

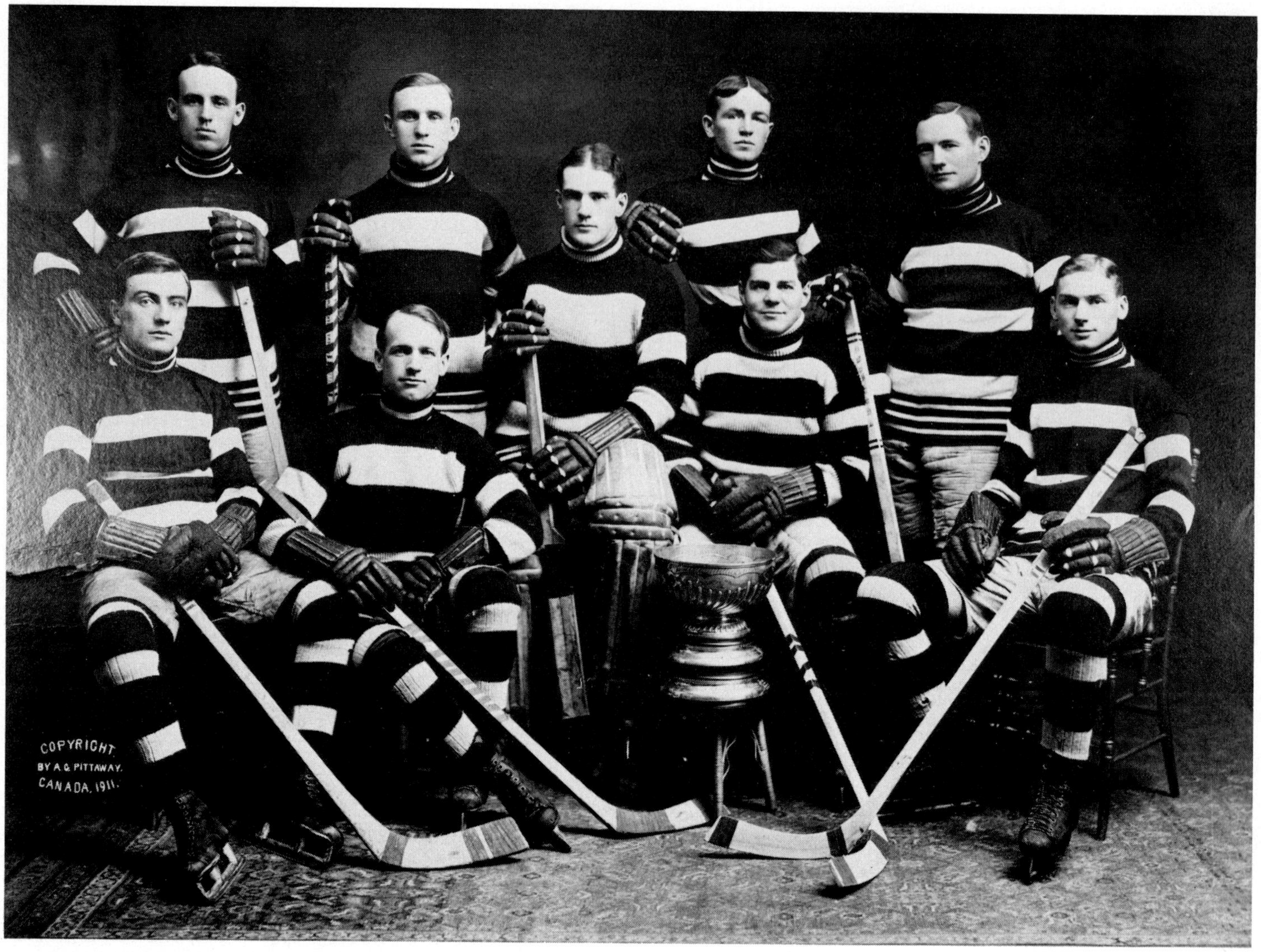

The Ottawa Senators, Stanley Cup champions, 1911.
HHF Archival Collection

The origin of the Montreal Canadiens might not seem relevant to the history of the Toronto Maple Leafs. Early on, however, there was an intimate connection between the two franchises. Historical investigation has revealed that the franchise which today is known as the Toronto Maple Leafs was in fact once known as the Montreal Canadiens. Following the first season of operation of the NHA, George Kennedy of the Club Athletique-Canadien in Montreal complained to NHA officials that the name "Les Canadiens" had been registered by his athletic club. Kennedy and his partners warned that if they were not awarded a franchise in the NHA, they would take action against the NHA for using their registered name. O'Brien agreed to transfer ownership of the Haileybury franchise to George Kennedy, along with the right to sign whatever players he wanted. Kennedy renamed the Haileybury franchise Les Canadiens, the NHA franchise that had played under the banner of Les Canadiens in 1910 having already been promised to a Toronto-based syndicate.

Kennedy hired most of the players from the 1910 Canadiens, since the Toronto syndicate did not yet have an arena and was not ready to ice a team. Toronto would not have been able to use most of the players anyway, since a league rule gave the exclusive signing rights of French-Canadian players to Montreal teams. From a distance, it looks like Les Canadiens had merely changed owners, but close examination reveals what actually happened: the Haileybury franchise had a new owner (George Kennedy's group), a new home town (Montreal), a new name (Les Canadiens), and new players, most of whom had played for "the 1910 Canadiens." But the papers giving Kennedy the rights to play in the league had previously belonged to Haileybury, not Montreal.

HOCKEY SERIES

ART. ROSS,
Sporting Goods Merchant,
Montreal,
Has played with
Brandon, 1905 to 1906
Kenora, 1907
Wanderers, 1908 to 1909
Haileybury, 1910

A Lancaster Reprint

HOCKEY SERIES

JOS. CATTARINICH,
Montreal,
Has played with
Montreal, 1907
Nationals, 1908 to 1909
Canadian, 1910

A Lancaster Reprint

HOCKEY SERIES

P. MORAN,
Quebec,
Has played with
All Montreal, 1909
Haileybury, 1910

A Lancaster Reprint

HOCKEY SERIES

D. PITRE,
Montreal,
Has played with
Michigan Soo, 1906
Shamrock, 1907 to 1908
Canadian Club, 1910

A Lancaster Reprint

HOCKEY SERIES

EDGAR DEY,
Ottawa,
Has played with
Portage La Prairie, 1906 to 1907
Pittsburg, 1908
Ottawa, 1909
Haileybury, 1910

A Lancaster Reprint

HOCKEY SERIES

J. LAVIOLETTE.
Montreal.
Has played with
Michigan Soo, 1906 to 1907
Shamrock, 1908 to 1909
Canadian Club 1910

A Lancaster Reprint

Haileybury, 1910. Following the 1910 season, the Haileybury franchise was sold to Montreal interests who renamed the team "Les Canadiens."

HHF Archival Collection

Montreal Canadiens, 1910. The team seen here wearing blue and white were the Montreal Canadiens in 1910. This franchise was sold to a Toronto group and was renamed the Toronto Blueshirts. In 1915 the team was renamed the Toronto Arenas, and in 1919 the Toronto St. Patricks, the immediate predecessors of the Toronto Maple Leafs.

HHF Archival Collection

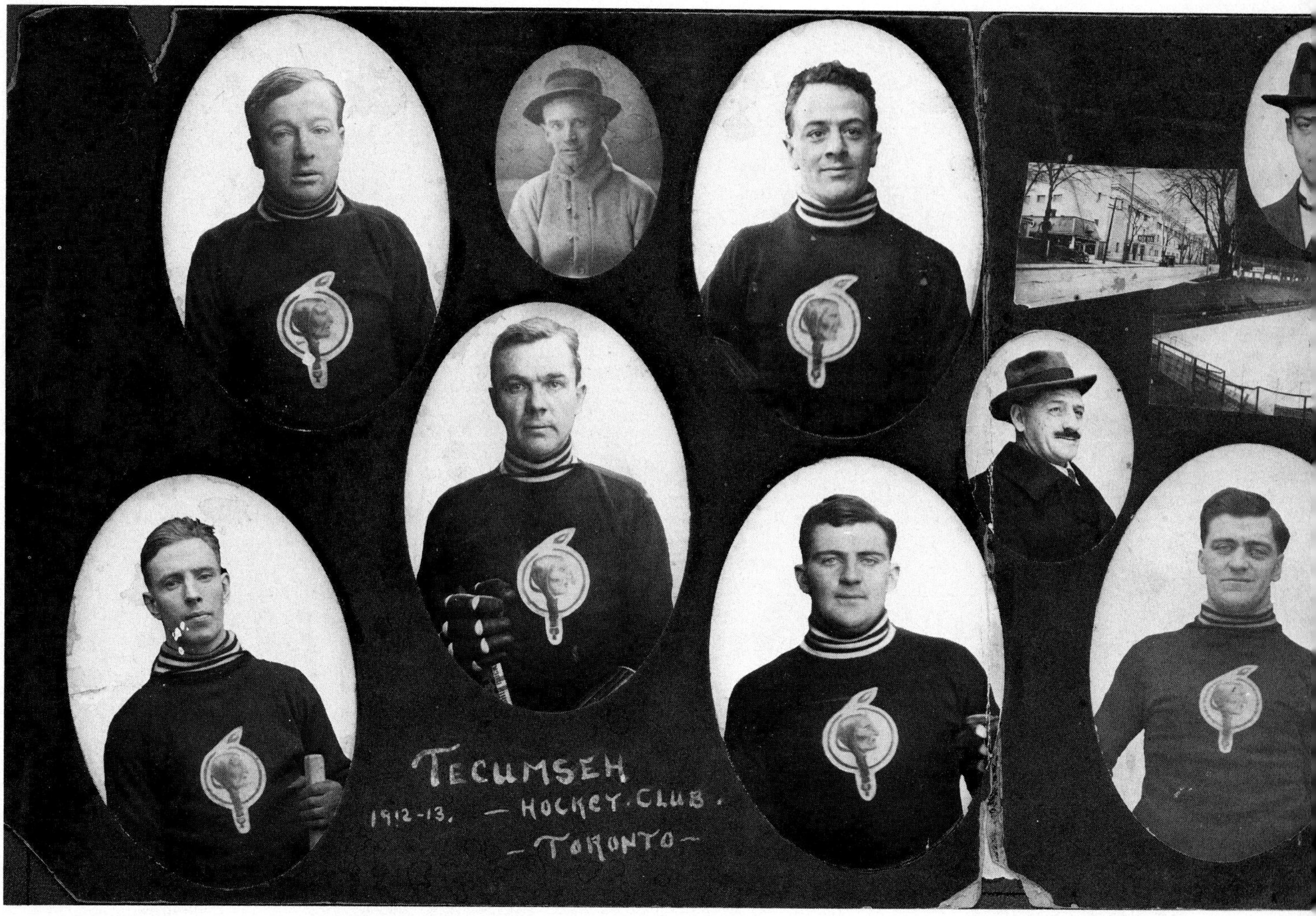

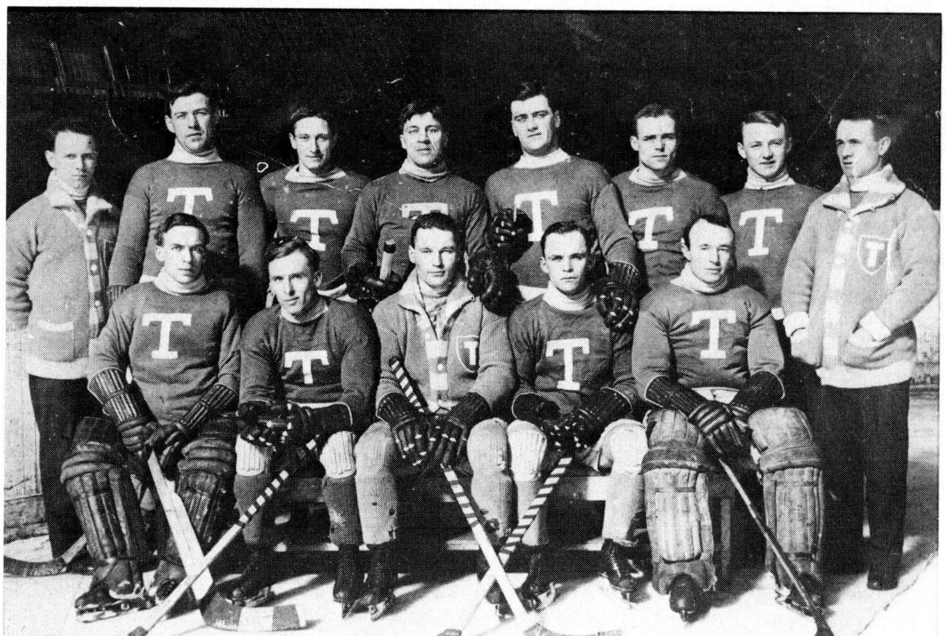

The Toronto Blueshirts, a powerhouse squad featuring Hall of Famers Hap Holmes, Harry Cameron, Frank Foyston, and Jack Marshall. In 1914 they became the first Toronto-based team to win the Stanley Cup.
HHF Archival Collection

The Toronto Tecumsehs, presided over by Charles Querrie, joined the National Hockey Association for the 1912–13 season. The Tecumsehs were renamed the Ontarios and then the Shamrocks before being amalgamated with the Blueshirts to form the Arenas.

HHF Archival Collection

The original NHA Montreal Canadiens franchise that played in 1910 was sold to the Toronto group on November 12, 1910; they did not ice a team until 1912, and when they did, it was under the banner of the Toronto Blueshirts. The complex trail of the Blueshirts reveals that this franchise eventually became the Toronto Maple Leafs. Even more ironic is the fact that the colours of the original 1910 Canadiens team were blue and white.

Though two Toronto interests had been awarded NHA franchises by 1911, it was not until the following year that teams were in place. The Toronto Blueshirts, under president Percy Quinn, and the Tecumsehs, under president Charlie Querrie, finished the NHA season in fourth and last place, respectively, in the six-team league. The Blueshirts, however, had some real talent that would soon pay dividends. Harry Holmes, Frank Nighbor, Frank Foyston, Harry Cameron, and Jack Marshall, all future members of the Hockey Hall of Fame, were all on the payroll in the 1912–13 season.

NHL president Clarence Campbell welcomes Frank Foyston into the Hockey Hall of Fame, 1958.

HHF Archival Collection

Duke Keats began his whirlwind hockey career with the Toronto Arenas in the 1916–17 season.
HHF Archival Collection

Cy Denneny began his professional career with the Toronto Shamrocks in 1914. He is seen here in his more familiar Ottawa jersey, which he wore from 1917 to 1928.
HHF Archival Collection

The following year (1913–14), the Blueshirts wound up tied for first place in the NHA with Kennedy's Montreal Canadiens. After downing the Canadiens in two games, the Blueshirts went on to play the Victoria Aristocrats of the new Pacific Coast Hockey Association (PCHA) for possession of the Stanley Cup. They swept Lester Patrick's Aristocrats in three games and brought the Cup to Toronto for the first time.

The 1914–15 season began a painful chapter in the history of professional hockey in Toronto. The Toronto Ontarios franchise (formerly the Tecumsehs) was purchased by E. J. (Eddie) Livingstone. He acquired the services of Donald Smith and Cy and Corbett Denneny and in mid-season changed the name of the team to the Shamrocks, in deference to the large Irish community in Toronto. He may have increased the take at the gate, but the Shamrocks finished fifth in the six-team league.

Not content with one franchise, the following season Livingstone purchased the Blueshirts from club owner (and NHA president) Frank Robinson, but ran into trouble when the league would not allow him to operate two franchises. While Livingstone was threatening to move the entire operation to Boston, the Patrick brothers of the PCHA swept in and made off with some of his best players (Cully Wilson, Corbett Denneny, Frank Foyston, and Harry Holmes). In desperation, Livingstone amalgamated the two franchises on November 20, 1915, and operated the empire under the banner of the Toronto Arenas.

More problems erupted for Livingstone when a new Toronto-based team joined the league. The Canadian Army's 228th Battalion was awarded a franchise to be comprised of sportsmen from that battalion. Among the enlisted men was Gordon "Duke" Keats, one of Livingstone's best players. While Livingstone wanted Keats to play for the Arenas, the army wanted him to play for the 228th. The army attempted to strongarm Livingstone by assigning Keats to guard duty whenever there was a game, but when the press got wind of the story, the public outcry resulted in Keats' playing for the Arenas.

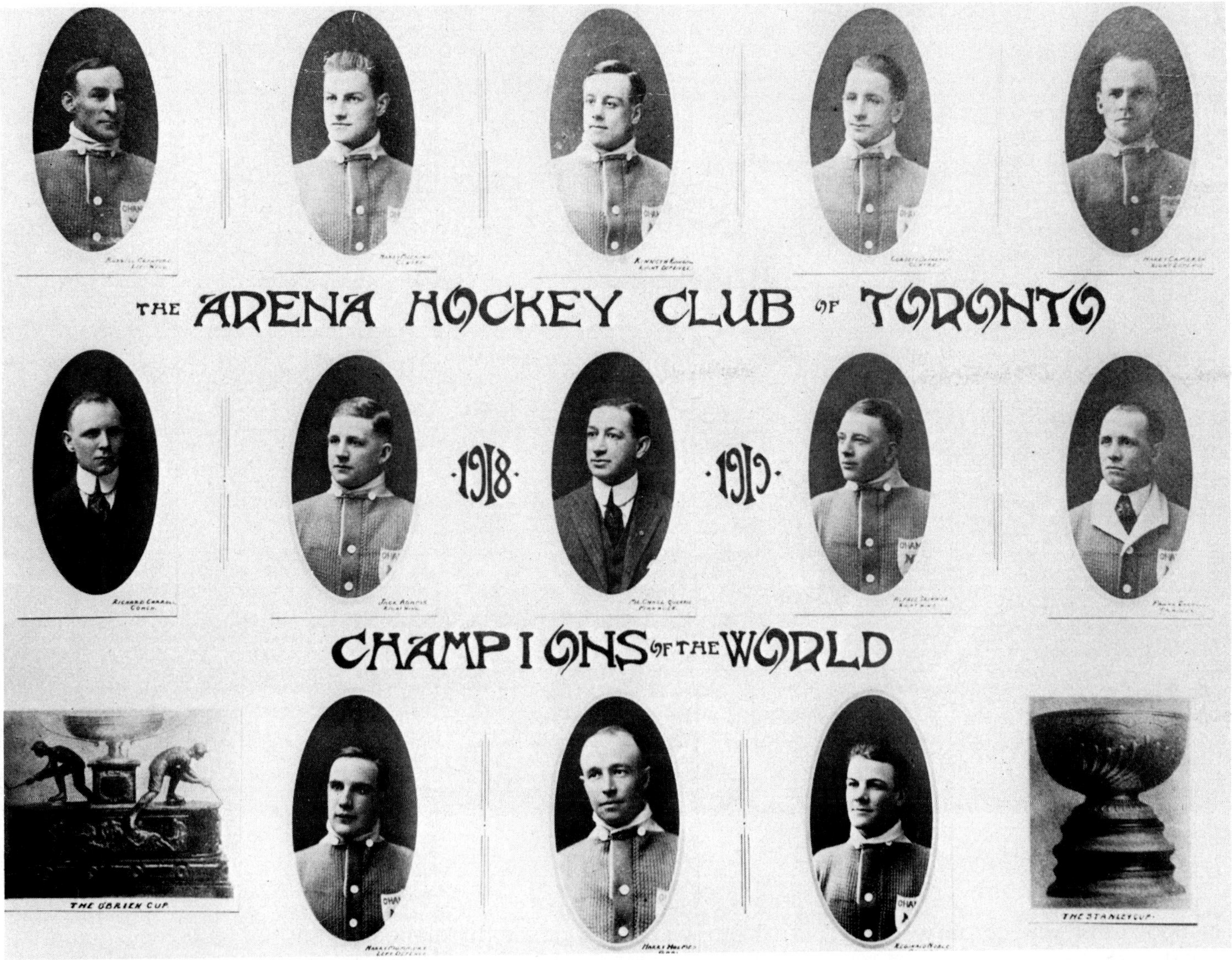

The Toronto Arenas. Following tumultuous boardroom battles, the National Hockey Association re-emerged in 1917 as the National Hockey League. The Toronto Arenas Hockey Club, which had been at the centre of the conflict, surfaced with the Stanley Cup in the spring of 1918.

HHF Archival Collection

Jack Adams is best known as the manager of one of Toronto's fiercest rivals, the Detroit Red Wings. Less well known is the fact that he began his big-league career in Toronto where he was a member of the 1917–18 Cup-winning Arenas.

HHF Archival Collection

Soon after, on February 10, 1917, the 228th was called overseas. Livingstone then demanded that the entire season be replayed — that the five remaining clubs play a double schedule. Livingstone's curmudgeonly behaviour over the Keats affair and now the call-ups was unpatriotic to say the least and angered NHA officials who not only refused to consider his request, but suspended the Toronto Arenas for the second half of the season.

By the fall of 1917 the NHA owners and directors were of one mind on the subject of Eddie Livingstone: the word that they would form a new league and freeze him out was on the street, but Livingstone was prepared for it. By November 9 he had sold his interests in the Arenas to the directors of the Toronto Arenas Company and appeared to be out of the picture. The NHA owners did indeed form a new league, the National Hockey League (NHL), on November 26, 1917. The Toronto Arenas were admitted on the understanding that Livingstone would have nothing whatsoever to do with the club. Charlie Querrie was to be coach and general manager. That there was a certain amount of subterfuge involved seems evident in that Livingstone was interfering from behind the scenes and Querrie threatened to quit unless he was guaranteed full control of the club.

Livingstone continued to be a thorn in the side of hockey officialdom for years, demanding justice for being ousted from the NHA/NHL and eventually suing the NHA and its members for conspiracy. In the end his suit amounted to nothing, the charter of the NHA having expired. Livingstone's departure from the Arenas had at least one memorable result: in 1918 the Toronto Arenas won the first Stanley Cup in the history of the NHL and the second in the long parade of Toronto's hockey heritage.

Despite their triumph the previous season, in 1918–19 the Arenas were powerless. In the first half of the season they lost seven of ten games, and although most of the matches were close, they found themselves at the bottom of the league. The second half was disastrous. They lost by scores of 10–0, 9–3, and 8–2. With two games left in the season, the Toronto Arenas threw in the towel, leaving the NHL with only two teams in competition.

The Arena owners realized that the team was due for some major renovations. They wiped the slate clean, starting the 1919–20 season with a new lineup and a new name — the Toronto St. Patricks.

Toronto St. Patricks, 1926–27. This is the team that on February 14, 1927, became the Toronto Maple Leafs. Seen at the right of the picture is coach Charles Querrie.
HHF Archival Collection

Babe Dye

When Babe Dye played with the Toronto St. Patricks in the 1920s, he was at his peak, and it was because his name was so well respected in the hockey world that he was, indirectly, the cause for the formation of the Toronto Maple Leafs Hockey Club. Conn Smythe had been hired by the newly formed New York Rangers to assemble a winning team for the 1926–27 season. He acquired a lot of good players, but he passed up the opportunity to sign three-time scoring champion Babe Dye. The New York sports press raised such a howl over Smythe's "incompetence" that Colonel John Hammond, owner of the Rangers, was forced to fire Smythe before his team ever cut NHL ice. So it was that Smythe was back in Toronto when the St. Pats went up on the block.

At the height of his career, Babe Dye set a record which is still among the foremost achievements in the game. In 1920–21 he scored 35 goals. While this is a respectable though not spectacular achievement in today's NHL, Dye did it in a 24-game season!

After being passed over by Smythe for the Rangers, Dye was sold to Chicago in 1926, where he played for two seasons. But he broke a leg in 1927 and his game never fully recovered. He moved from Chicago to hockey's last stand, the New York Americans, where his playing was merely adequate. In 1930 he returned to Toronto but played only six games, ending his on-ice career where it began 11 years earlier. He was elected to the Hockey Hall of Fame in 1970.

John Ross Roach played for the Toronto St. Pats/Maple Leafs from 1921 to 1928 before being traded to the Rangers.

HHF Archival Collection

The Toronto St. Pats skated out onto the ice on December 27, 1919, with a new look and a strong lineup. Vern Forbes replaced Bert Lindsay in goal, Reg Noble came up from the Toronto Riverdales of the OHA, Corbett Denneny returned from the Pacific Coast league, and Babe Dye and Mickey Roach were the "rooks." To ensure that this new team would not be roughed up, the St. Pats brought back their enforcer, Cully Wilson, fresh from a suspension in the PCHA for rearranging the facial features of Lloyd Cook and "Gentleman" Mickey MacKay. During the season, the St. Pats set an NHL attendance record when more than 8500 fans attended a game against the Ottawa Senators. The team was also part of a record on the other side of the ledger when Joe Malone of the Quebec Bulldogs scored seven goals in a single game on January 31, 1920, against the St. Pats, an NHL record that stands to this day. The St. Pats ended with a respectable 12–12–0 record and stood third overall in the four-team league.

The St. Pats continued to improve in the 1920–21 campaign. After a 5–5–0 first half, they rose to first place, finishing the second half with a 10–4–0 record. The Hamilton Tigers were a new entry in 1920, and the St. Pats spotted them some decent talent to spice up the competition. Babe Dye, Goldie Prodgers, and Joe Matte went to Hamilton, but Dye got homesick for Toronto after only one game and appeared for the St. Pats the following night. The St. Pats were glad he did: Dye found the mark 35 times that season and led not only his team but the entire league in scoring. The St. Pats advanced to the playoffs against Ottawa, where the superior Senators vanquished them in two games without allowing a single Toronto goal.

The following season (1921–22) the St. Pats' new coach, Eddie Powers, added John Ross Roach as their goaltender, and with his steady play the team

John Ross Roach

The Maple Leafs' first goalie was originally signed to play for the St. Pats at the age of 21. John Ross Roach was renowned for the nervous energy that kept him pacing through most of the game. He was often referred to as "The Housecleaner" because he was always sweeping out his crease area, keeping it clear of snow.

Roach first appeared in goal for the St. Pats in the 1921–22 season. Although his statistics that winter were poor, when the spring season began, Roach improved dramatically. He recorded two post-season zeros in leading the St. Pats past both the defending Cup champions, the Ottawa Senators, and the challengers from the West Coast, the Vancouver Millionaires. The St. Pats never won the Stanley Cup again, but when Conn Smythe bought the team, he kept Roach in the cage for the Leafs.

Roach's tenure in Toronto was highly impressive, at least on paper. He lowered his goals-against average for six of the seven winters he spent with the St. Pats and Leafs and recorded 13 shutouts. When Lorne Chabot became available, Smythe traded Roach to the Rangers, where he had his finest years.

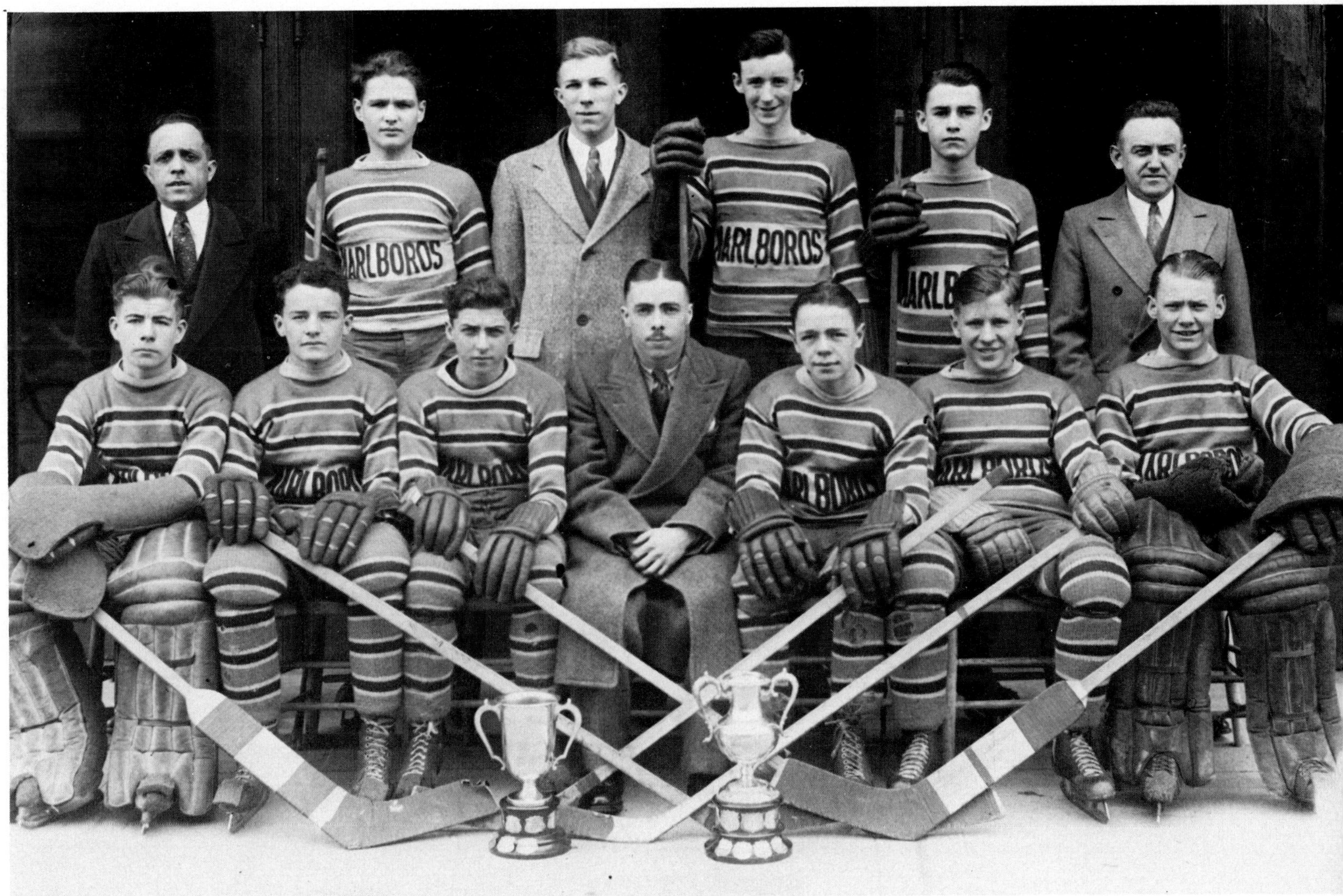

Toronto Marlboros, ca. 1924. The Marlboros were organized by Frank Selke during the twenties with the aid of Conn Smythe. Selke resurrected the name from the original Marlboroughs who by this time were defunct. Selke proved his worth first with the Marlboros and later with Toronto and the Montreal Canadiens as an astute manager and scout. The Marlboros went on to become the single most important farm club for the Toronto Maple Leafs.

HHF Archival Collection

finished the season with a 13–10–1 record. Babe Dye was among the top scorers in the league again, and with newcomers Kenny Randall and Dr. Rod Smylie, the team went on to meet the Ottawa Senators once again in the NHL playoffs. This time the St. Pats exacted their revenge, ousting the Senators 5 goals to 4 in the total-goals series. When the NHL champions met the PCHA champions for possession of the Stanley Cup, Toronto was ready. Babe Dye scored nine goals, and with timely markers coming from Corbett Denneny and Smylie, the St. Pats downed the Vancouver Millionaires in five games and received their first Stanley Cup, the third in the history of the city.

The St. Pats finished the 1922–23 season with the same record as in the previous year but were bumped from the playoff roster on the final day of the season, when Montreal won over Hamilton. Prior to the start of the 1922–23 schedule, Eddie Powers moved to Boston to coach the Westminsters, who had been New England champions in 1922. Charlie Querrie took over the coaching duties once again, and dealt Corbett Denneny to Vancouver in exchange for Jolly Jack Adams. After only six games, Adams took over the coaching from Querrie, who had his hands full managing the club. The St. Pats were negotiating to sign young superstar Hooley Smith, but they were unwilling to meet his salary demands. Smith was bold enough to suggest that they drop Jack Adams and Reg Noble and put their paycheques in his pocket! Querrie decided against the deal and Smith did not play for Toronto. On a positive note, Babe Dye led the league in scoring for the second time.

Red Stewart and Amos Arbour are valuable commodities in the hockey card collectors' market. Of special note is the "World Champions" patch that all members of the 1923–24 St. Patricks team sported.

Hayes Collection, HHF

Eddie Powers returned from New England in 1923–24 to coach the St. Pats once again. Though the team was glad to see him back, he could not restore the fortunes of the dethroned heroes. The St. Pats stumbled to a 10–14–0 low-water mark, allowing 85 goals in only 24 games. Needless to say, they didn't make the 1924 playoffs.

Eddie Powers moved into the St. Pats' front office in 1924–25, filling the dual role of coach/general manager. Before leaving the organization, Charlie Querrie had discovered Hap Day, a young pharmacy student who played with Conn Smythe's University of Toronto team. Querrie persuaded Day to spend his nights at the big rink, where his talents were put to good use. The St. Pats finished the 1924–25 NHL season in second place, one point behind the Hamilton Tigers, and Babe Dye was again top goal scorer in the NHL. Then, a players' strike in Hamilton led to the Tigers' suspension from the league, so that the St. Pats met the Montreal Canadiens in the NHL playoffs, but Toronto lost the total-goals series 5 goals to 2.

After coaching the Toronto St. Pats to the Stanley Cup in 1922, Eddie Powers, pictured here in about 1923, became the bench boss for the Boston Westminsters but returned the following season to his spot behind the St. Patricks' bench.

HHF Archival Collection

Toronto St. Patricks 1923–24. The St. Pats of 1923–24 finished third in the four-team NHL. Hockey Hall of Famers Jack Adams and Babe Dye are at front row centre.

HHF Archival Collection

Hap Day

The first great Leaf defenceman actually began his professional career as a left winger. Clarence Henry "Hap" Day was spotted by Charlie Querrie, general manager of the St. Pats, while he was playing senior hockey for the Hamilton Tigers. At this time, Day was also studying pharmacy at the University of Toronto. Conn Smythe wanted Day to join his Varsity Grads team, and Hap actually suited up for a couple of matches, but the lure of cash and a professional career convinced him to sign with the St. Pats.

Day made his NHL debut in 1924, playing left wing and scoring a respectable 10 goals in his rookie campaign. When Smythe purchased the St. Pats in February 1927, he finally had his man. There's no disputing Smythe's judgment of talent and of men: his first managerial moves were to switch Day from left wing to the blueline, where he had played throughout his amateur career, and to make him the Leafs first captain. The moves paid instant dividends for the newly formed Maple Leafs. Day anchored the Leaf defence for another 10 seasons, serving as captain throughout his career in the blue and white. On November 19, 1929, in a game against the Pittsburgh Pirates, Day scored 4 goals — a record for a defenceman that stood until another Leaf blueliner, Ian Turnbull, broke it in 1977.

On April 5, 1932, Hap Day fired the first goal ever scored by the Leafs in the Stanley Cup finals, leading his squad to their first Cup victory. Happy Day was sold to the New York Americans before the 1937–38 season, ending his 13-year playing career in Toronto. He returned to Toronto as coach from 1940 to 1950 and then managed the Leafs until 1957. He was elected to the Hockey Hall of Fame, as a player, in 1961.

The Tobacco Products Corporation of Hamilton, Ontario, issued this collection of hockey cards in 1924. These cards, among the rarest in existence, were probably issued before the season began, as Mickey O'Leary never seems to have made this or any other big-league team, and Stanton Jackson was traded after only a few games.
Hayes Collection, HHF

The St. Pats were plagued by injuries during the 1925–26 season and finished with an ignominious 12–21–3 record. At the peak of their frustration, they were forced to forfeit a game on February 27 against the Canadiens. After a bloody brawl which included players, fans, police, and officials, Captain Babe Dye took the puck (the only puck on the premises) and refused to give it back to referee Bobby Hewitson. Hewitson blew the whistle on these shenanigans, packed up his skates, and went home, awarding the victory to Montreal.

The 1926–27 season began with Mike Rodden behind the St. Pats' bench and a revised lineup. Babe Dye and Jack Adams were sold to Chicago, and Ace Bailey was acquired from Peterborough of the OHA senior league. The St. Pats had some talented men — notably Bailey and Day — but they were floundering. There seemed to be a malaise that kept the players from coming together as a unit. The team's popularity and profitability was dwindling; owner Jack Bickell saw that things were falling apart and put the Toronto St. Patricks up for sale in the fall of 1926.

The NHL at this time was expanding into the United States and Bickell had a fair offer of $200,000 from interests in Philadelphia. After the Hamilton players' strike over the 1925 playoffs, the Tigers franchise was moved to New York and became the Americans. New York City had also acquired another NHL franchise and assembled a top-notch team to begin play as the New York Rangers in the 1926–27 season.

Conn Smythe had been courted by the new owners of the Rangers to scout, sign, build, and manage the new team. Smythe was a businessman and sportsman who had captained the University of Toronto Varsity hockey team that won the Ontario championship in 1915. Since the end of the Great

Reginald "Hooley" Smith was a member of the Granites, the team that won the Olympic hockey championship for Canada in 1924. He was a top-notch prospect, and Charlie Querrie was eager to sign him to the St. Pats. But they couldn't agree on salary, so Smith was picked up by the Ottawa Senators instead.

Imperial Oil Turofsky Collection, HHF

Ace Bailey

The Ace Bailey story serves to illustrate both the dark side of hockey and the deep-seated camaraderie and sportsmanship that are very much a part of the game. Bailey was brought up as a rookie to the St. Pats in 1926. By 1929 he was the league's top point getter — the first Leaf to win that honour — with 22 goals and 10 assists in the 44-game season. He was a main attraction and Toronto's featured star when, in a game at the Boston Garden on December 12, 1933, he was seriously injured in a vicious attack by the bad boy of the league, Boston's Eddie Shore.

Shore had been checked hard and knocked senseless by King Clancy. He was delirious and furious when he scrambled back to his feet, and he went after the first blue and white blur in sight. Unfortunately for Ace Bailey, he was that blur. Shore hit Bailey from behind with such ferocity that Bailey was lifted off his feet and crashed to the ice head first. He was cold and bleeding when the team skated to his side. Shore himself was badly injured in a retaliatory action by Red Horner, but he recovered completely. Ace's death notice appeared in the morning papers in Boston, but though his life hung in the balance for days, he did not die. His career, however, was over, and the game of ice hockey would never be quite the same.

February 14, 1934, was Ace Bailey Night at Maple Leaf Gardens. Players from around the league gave freely of their time to form an all-star team and challenge Toronto in a benefit game which marked the beginning of the NHL's all-star tradition. Shore and Bailey appeared at centre ice, and with a handshake and a smile, the matter between them was closed.

During his eight seasons with the Toronto club, Bailey had been a resolute and stellar player, and his sweater, Number 6, was retired in his honour. Bailey did not leave the Gardens, however; he held the post of timekeeper for the next several decades. During that time he saw a lot of players come and go, but none impressed him more than the young Ron Ellis. More than 30 years after the dreadful incident that ended his own career, Bailey requested that Number 6 be brought out of retirement and given to Ron Ellis.

Ace Bailey was elected to the Hockey Hall of Fame in 1975.

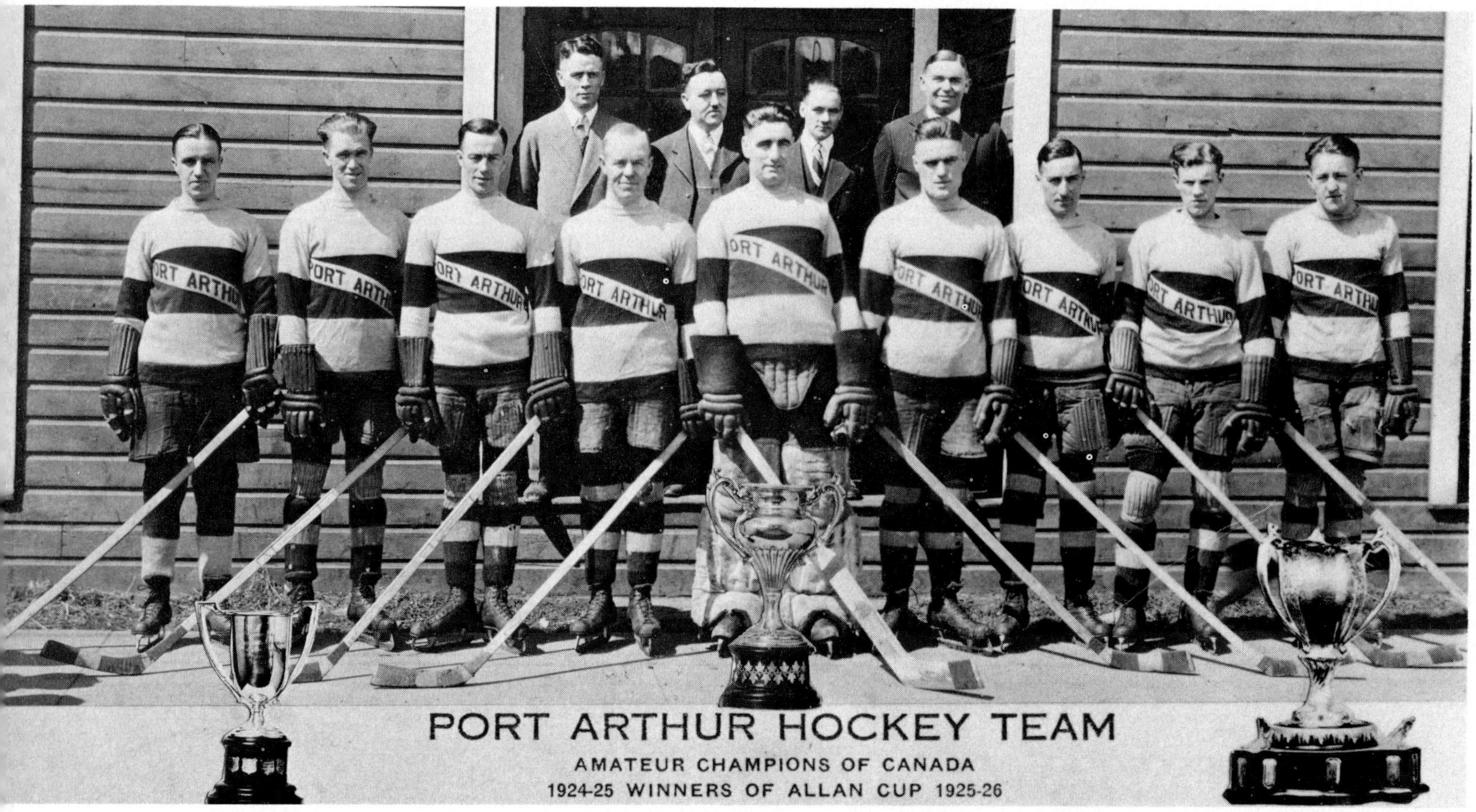

When Conn Smythe was scouting for the New York Rangers, he found goalie Lorne Chabot in Port Arthur, Ontario, playing for the Bear Cats. Chabot played in New York for a couple of years until he stopped a Howie Morenz blast with his face. Rangers manager Les Patrick figured Chabot was pretty much washed up, but Smythe, now owner of the Leafs, had faith in Chabot, and traded John Ross Roach to the Rangers to get him. "Chabotsky" came back to haunt Patrick when in 1932 the Leafs swept the Rangers in the Cup final, and Chabot registered a 2.14 average.

Imperial Oil Turofsky Collection, HHF

War he had returned to the university to complete his education, married and had three children, built up a successful sand and gravel company, and acquired several racehorses while continuing his involvement with hockey as coach of the Varsity team and an investor in Frank Selke's Toronto Marlboros. In 1918 Smythe met Frank Selke who was coach of the St. Mary's Juniors, a fine amateur team from one of Toronto's Catholic schools. Both men were in their early thirties and had been involved in hockey virtually all their lives. It was natural that they should become friends. Selke started a minor professional team of his own in the OHA in 1924, reviving the Marlboroughs name — now spelt Marlboros — from Toronto's turn-of-the-century hockey club. He assembled various financial backers for the new venture, one of whom was Conn Smythe.

By the mid-twenties Smythe had become fairly well known around race tracks, boxing rings, poker games, and of course hockey rinks, and he was snapped up by Colonel John Hammond, the major power behind the New York Rangers. They were kindred spirits — tough, no-nonsense businessmen, sportsmen, and war heroes who knew how to bet and how to win. Smythe knew that he was not likely to find the kind of future stars he wanted to manage for the Rangers hanging around the rinks in National Hockey League towns. He looked hard at players in the backwater leagues and small towns, and seemed to pay little heed to the hockey politics of the day. This attitude proved unpopular with the New York sports press and the Rangers' management, but future events attested to Smythe's unerring instinct for nosing out hockey talent. He came up with Ching Johnson and Taffy Able while on a swing through Minnesota, even though there was a gentlemen's agreement that players from that state were property of the western circuit. He acquired Lorne Chabot from the Allan Cup winning Port Arthur squad in northern Ontario and

Babe Dye, a three-time scoring leader in the NHL and captain of the Toronto St. Patricks, was available to Smythe when he was putting together the Rangers team. Smythe, for reasons known only to himself, would not sign the Babe to a Ranger contract, and the New York press gave the Rangers ownership such a hellish time over Smythe's "incompetence" that the Rangers let Smythe go. Dye went to Chicago and never performed as an all-star again.
Imperial Oil Turofsky Collection, HHF

Lorne Chabot

Even though his career with the Leafs was a fairly short one, Lorne Chabot, in backstopping the Toronto Maple Leafs to their first Stanley Cup victory, is as important to club history as any man who ever tended goal for the team.

When Conn Smythe was hired to build the New York Rangers, the goaltender he chose was the beetle-browed Chabot from the Port Arthur squad, who had almost single-handedly defeated Smythe's Varsity Grads in the 1925 Allan Cup Final. Chabot spent two seasons guarding the gate at Madison Square Garden, but after he suffered an eye injury the Rangers gave up on him, and Smythe jumped at the chance to acquire the veteran for his youthful Leaf squad. The Leafs made the playoffs for the first time and, though they eventually lost to the Rangers, Chabot allowed only five goals in four games. In the 1929–30 schedule, "Chabotsky" registered more zeros than any competing goaltender, setting the stage for even greater on-ice success.

In 1932 the Leafs met the Rangers in the Stanley Cup finals, and both Chabot and Smythe took special pride when the Leafs defeated the Broadway Blues for their first Cup victory. Arguably, Chabot's greatest post-season performance came during the semi-finals of 1933. In the decisive fifth game, Chabot kept the Bruins off the scoreboard for the better part of nine periods as the Leafs captured a 1–0 decision after six overtime frames. The Leafs succumbed to the Rangers in the finals that year, but Chabot's performance still ranks as one of the greatest in Stanley Cup legend.

After the 1932–33 season, Chabot was traded to the Montreal Canadiens, but he continued to excel in NHL arenas until he retired in 1937.

Colonel John Hammond (right), owner of the New York Rangers, and Lester Patrick, ca. 1928. Patrick was hired by Hammond to coach the Rangers after he had fired Conn Smythe.
Imperial Oil Turofsky Collection, HHF

brought three high-class professionals — Bill Cook, Bun Cook, and Frank Boucher — from the Western Canada League (WCL) and the PCHA to play in New York.

Sixty-five years later we can only doff our caps to Smythe's uncanny scouting skill, but at the time, the New York press was grilling him. The acquisition of "no-name players" and "tired western skaters" elicited hoots in the daily papers. Smythe's refusal to purchase Babe Dye, a four-time NHL scoring champion and captain of the Toronto St. Patricks, brought down such wrath that Hammond had little choice but to send him packing before the season got under way.

Smythe returned to Toronto to coach the University of Toronto Varsity team once again — they won the Allan Cup that year, and in 1928, under the moniker "Varsity Grads," and with Smythe still coaching, they took the Olympic title as well.

Hammond had paid Smythe three-quarters of his $10,000 contract, and hired Lester Patrick to fill the job. In 1911 Lester and his brother Frank Patrick had founded the Pacific Coast Hockey Association, bankrolled by their father, a successful lumber baron. It had been immensely successful, but by 1926 it could no longer compete with the expanding NHL. Smythe was not the only one raiding into the western leagues. In what was the biggest deal in hockey up to that time the Patricks sold their entire league to NHL interests in September 1926. Lester Patrick moved back east to manage Hammond's Rangers — the players Smythe had assembled "by hook or by crook," some of them pirated from Patrick's PCHA territory.

Smythe, meanwhile, was determined to have the rest of his Rangers contract money. He went over Hammond's head to Tex Rickard, owner of the Rangers' new home, Madison Square Garden. He

Conn Smythe (right) outside the entrance to the Mutual Street Arena ca. 1933. "Conn Smythe didn't mind us having a beer, but not whisky. 'You'll ruin your organs,' he would say. 'Have your beer, stop at two.' He was a good man to play for. He never forgot you if you produced."
— Ace Bailey
Imperial Oil Turofsky Collection, HHF

impressed Rickard, reportedly with his ability to pick winners in games between the Rangers and the current Cup champions, the Montreal Maroons, and by betting on Gene Tunney to win the boxing title. Rickard even offered Smythe the vice-presidency of the Rangers organization before he learned of the dispute with Hammond. But by this time Smythe had other irons in the fire. He scooped up his $2500 and went off to Montreal where the University of Toronto football team was playing McGill University. He put the $2500 down on Toronto to win — and doubled his money. Knowing he was on a roll, he then bet the entire $5000 on the Rangers to win over the Toronto St. Patricks, and doubled his money again. With a spring in his step, he took his winnings and went looking for a bigger challenge and a higher stakes game.

Smythe made a laughable offer to purchase the St. Patricks with $10,000 down. Jack Bickell was faced with a choice between Smythe's pittance and the $200,000 offer from Philadelphia. With very little time to stall the American offer, Smythe raised $160,000 — and the Canadian flag. With his hand on his heart and his eyes at attention, he appealed to Bickell's sense of national pride and his honour as a great Canadian business leader, pleading for the future of hockey in Toronto. Bickell, against all odds, left his own money in the team on condition that Smythe run the club himself.

The Toronto Granites, Olympic champions, 1924.
HHF Archival Collection

Bill Carson's career as a Maple Leaf was fairly brief, but he holds a unique spot in the team history. On November 15, 1927, he scored the first goal for the Leafs in their first full season.
Imperial Oil Turofsky Collection, HHF

Conn Smythe was not a follower. He was the sort of man to leave his imprint in the hardest of pavement, and it would not do to have the new team continue as the St. Patricks. Among the teams he scouted for talent were a group of young men who called themselves the East Toronto Maple Leafs. Smythe liked the name. He liked that the maple leaf was something of a Canadian symbol, that it was the logo of the 1924 Olympic team, and that he had worn it proudly as a soldier in the Great War. It would be the symbol of his proud new team. Smythe designed new uniforms for the squad, but he kept the green colour for one more season, as a sign of respect for the loyal supporters of the St. Pats team. On February 14, 1927, the Toronto Maple Leafs were born.

Smythe could have stepped in behind the bench to coach his new team, but he knew that his talents were needed elsewhere. He was busy with the Varsity team — this was the year he took them to the Allan Cup — so he appointed Alex Romeril as manager, and he kibitzed from the sidelines. His first move was to order Hap Day from forward to defence, and Day was to captain the team from behind

Art Duncan played for the Leafs from 1927–1931 and stayed on briefly as coach before being replaced by Dick Irvin in the 1931–32 season.
Imperial Oil Turofsky Collection, HHF

Carl Voss was the first player acquired by Conn Smythe for the new Toronto Maple Leafs.
Imperial Oil Turofsky Collection, HHF

the blueline. Ironically, the first player Smythe signed to the new team to wear that most Canadian of team logos was an American, Carl Voss. Voss played only 14 games for the Leafs, but when he resurfaced with Detroit in 1932, he was named Rookie of the Year. The Leafs finished in last place in the spring of 1927 with a 15–24–5 record, but with the new ownership in place, and Smythe out on the scouting trail, the future looked promising for the fledgling team.

For the 1927–28 season Smythe added Art Duncan from the Detroit Cougars (recently Lester Patrick's Victoria Cougars and later the Red Wings) and purchased Jimmy Herberts from Boston for $12,000. He was quick to realize that Herberts wasn't worth the investment, and with very little cash to throw around, led the Detroit management to believe that Herberts was a burgeoning superstar, but that the Leafs needed money and would part with Herberts for the bargain price of $15,000. The Cougars were skeptical. Smythe explained that Herberts' wife was not happy in Toronto; she yearned to return to her home town of Windsor, Ontario, just across the river from Detroit. Then,

Harold Cotton came up into the National League with the Pittsburgh Pirates in 1925. Though built like a defenceman, Cotton had all the skills necessary to make a good forward liner: he was a fast skater, an accurate playmaker, and able to score when the spirit moved him. "Baldy," as he was known, played for the Leafs from 1928 to 1935.

Imperial Oil Turofsky Collection, HHF

when the Cougars' bagmen arrived to have a look at Herberts, Smythe instructed his men to set up Herberts at every opportunity. Herberts performed exceedingly well and the next morning Smythe laughed all the way to the bank, where he deposited the $15,000 he needed to meet his payroll.

Conn Smythe was a natural leader and would not ask his subordinates to do anything he wouldn't do himself — including engaging in physical encounters. In a March 24 tilt against the Montreal Maroons, when shooting and scoring turned to punching and smacking, he set a precedent he would follow on many future occasions: he was out there with his boys, slugging it out.

Despite finishing the 1927–28 campaign with an 18–18–8 mark, and missing the playoffs, Smythe had begun to brew his winning team. He had found young Joe Primeau thanks to Frank Selke while scouting for the Rangers, and had signed him to a personal contract. During the off season of 1928, he traded John Ross Roach and Butch Keeling to the Rangers for Lorne Chabot, purchased Harold "Baldy" Cotton from Pittsburgh, added Andy Blair from the Allan Cup winning Winnipeg team, and brought up Red Horner from Frank Selke's junior Marlboros. He felt his squad was strong enough to

Red Horner

The first scouting report on Red Horner, supplied by Shrimp McPherson, ran something like this: "Oh, he'll get you a lot of penalties . . . he has his elbow in your kisser and his fanny in your tummy all the time he's on the ice." Those words pretty well sum up the style of the man commonly regarded as the NHL's first "enforcer."

Red Horner was "discovered" by Marlboro manager Frank Selke. He was Selke's paperboy and pestered Selke to let him try out with the newly re-formed Toronto Marlboros. It was at the Marlboros' initial practice in 1926 that McPherson spotted him. Selke signed the rabble-rouser, and that season the Marlies went to the Eastern Canadian Finals. The next season Conn Smythe called Horner to join the Leafs where he remained in the lineup until he retired 12 years later, serving two terms as captain, from 1938 to 1940.

Horner was a rough player who gave no quarter and expected none. He led the NHL in penalty time for eight straight seasons, though his accumulation of minutes seems tame by today's standards. Despite his "bad man" image, Horner was respected by both the fans and his opponents. He was a clean player who never used his stick to make a point and took his place in the box without protest. More than anything, Horner's ferocious body-checking characterized his on-ice flair; it's been said that if Horner laid the body on you on a Saturday night, your head wouldn't clear until Tuesday.

Smythe summed up Horner's career best, calling him "the inspirational force behind the Leaf teams of the 1930s." Red Horner was accorded the ultimate honour by his peers when he was elected to the Hockey Hall of Fame in 1965.

In the summer of 1931, scout Squib Walker signed Frank "Buzz" Boll, a young kid from Filmore, Saskatchewan, to an option contract, and brought him to Toronto to meet Smythe. Boll had played with the Regina Pats and was a very hot prospect among the scouting coterie. To keep him in Toronto and out of the grasp of the competition, Smythe set him up with a job as a night watchman at the Gardens site. The ploy worked and Buzz signed with the Leafs.

Imperial Oil Turofsky Collection, HHF

allow Joe Primeau a year of seasoning in the minors, and sent him to London, Ontario.

Smythe was on his way to building a winner. The success of the Rangers squad he assembled proved that he was capable, but his Leafs were not quite Stanley Cup calibre yet. They made the 1929 playoffs, but lost to the Rangers in two closely fought games in the second round.

On the record books, the 1929–30 outing does not appear to be a banner year for the Leafs, but six decades later it's clear that this building year was as significant as any in Maple Leaf history. In September Frank Selke joined the organization as Smythe's full-time assistant to help manage, scout, and promote the new team. Smythe brought up a couple of young kids, Charlie Conacher and Busher Jackson,

Charlie Conacher

When Charlie Conacher, one of a great family of Ontario athletes, came up to play for the Maple Leafs in 1929, he gave Toronto hockey fans a notion of what was to come. In his first game the 19-year-old Torontonian found the mark, and he scored 19 more goals before the season ended. The following year he was NHL scoring champion and in 1932 led the Leafs to the Stanley Cup. "The Big Bomber" led the NHL in goals scored on five occasions and won the Art Ross Trophy twice. During his nine years with the team, the Leafs won the Cup once and the league championship twice.

It is often said that big goal scorers have soft hands, and in Conacher's case this was true. Though he outscored most of his contemporaries while he was with the Leafs, he did so despite an infected hand in 1930, and a broken hand in 1931, 1932, and 1936. Considering that he also suffered several shoulder dislocations as well as problems with his feet, we can only wonder what he might have done were he whole and sound throughout.

Charlie Conacher is best remembered as a member of that most dynamic assembly of Leaf forwards, the Kid Line, along with Harvey "Busher" Jackson and Joe Primeau. This line of young blood scored at will, and were the most fearsome trio of the thirties. In the Stanley Cup winning year of 1931–32 Jackson, Primeau, and Conacher finished first, second, and fourth in the scoring race.

By 1938 Conacher's heyday was past. He went to Detroit for a season, and finally to New York where he played defence with Eddie Shore for the Americans. Later he coached the Chicago Blackhawks from 1947 to 1950. Conacher was inducted into the Hockey Hall of Fame in 1961.

Andy Blair joined up with the Leafs for the 1928–29 season and did regular service for the team as a centreman till the mid-thirties. In his 358 games with the Maple Leafs, Blair scored 74 goals and helped on 83 more for a points total of 157 over his eight-year stint.

HHF Archival Collection

When Alex Levinsky joined the Leafs in 1931, he was one of the very few American-born players to skate in the NHL, and he was the only Jewish player in hockey. His solid blueline work helped the Leafs to the Stanley Cup in 1932.

Imperial Oil Turofsky Collection, HHF

Art Duncan, coach of the Maple Leafs, welcomes King Clancy to the club in 1930. Duncan (left), lasted only five games into the 1932 season. Clancy stayed with the club for 56 years.

Imperial Oil Turofsky Collection, HHF

from the Marlboros team, and on December 29, 1929, sent them out on a line with a slumping Joe Primeau. The Kid Line was born. The Leafs added another important link in the chain of success when they traded Danny Cox to Ottawa for the aging Frank Nighbor. Smythe now had a good mixture of young blood and seasoned veterans, but the Leafs were still allowing more goals than they were scoring, and if they were to be serious contenders, they would need a solid blueliner to stop the attackers cold.

Looking around the league in the summer of 1930, Smythe saw a couple of good prospects, but his best bet by far was a feisty little guy on the Ottawa roster. Although their lineup was one of the best in the league, Ottawa had financial trouble. They were desperate enough to put their best player on the block — at the unheard-of price of $35,000. The high price tag may have been enough in itself to interest Smythe: the challenge of finding 35,000 depression dollars for one sawed-off defenceman was more than he could resist. When he brought the prospect of buying King Clancy to the Leafs' board of directors, they were prepared to pay only the first $25,000. If Smythe wanted Clancy, he would have to find the rest himself. He got the money the best way he knew how: he gambled for it.

Smythe owned a race horse called Rare Jewel, whom he entered in the Coronation Futurity. She had a poor track record, which meant high odds, and Smythe bet heavily to win, both at the track and off. The luck of the Irish was with him: Rare Jewel wore number 7 and she was number 11 on the pole. She had one other advantage — she was drunk, having been given a pint of brandy prior to the race. When the dust cleared, it was Rare Jewel by a nose. Smythe made the rounds at the wickets and picked up the balance of funds he needed to buy King Clancy.

King Clancy

In the 1920s the Ottawa Senators were the major hockey attraction. People came out in droves to see them in all NHL towns — except Ottawa. Owing to this quirk of their hometown box office, the Senators were in financial straits, so they decided to cash in on their most valuable asset — King Clancy.

When Conn Smythe heard that the unprecedented sum of $35,000 was the asking price for the diminutive defenceman, he set out to get it. His board scoffed at the figure, allowing him no more than $25,000. Smythe picked up the rest at the race track, betting on his own filly — Rare Jewel — who had been saving herself till now. Owing to her poor performance thus far, Rare Jewel was a longshot, and her win financed the greatest deal in the Leafs' trading history.

Clancy was a little guy by any standard, but he never shirked his defence responsibilities, going after the biggest bruisers of his day. What he lacked in stature, he made up for in skill, cunning, and devilry. As the King used to say, "I don't finish fights, I just start 'em." In a game against Boston, Clancy tripped Eddie Shore, unnoticed by the referee; Clancy then tiptoed up to Shore and whispered in his ear: "Jeeze, Eddie, that was a blatant foul; I'd really give the referee what for on that one." Toronto was down at the time, but after Shore spent 14 minutes in the sin bin for bad-mouthing the referee, the Leafs had salted away a tidy win.

After Clancy retired from the team in November 1936, the NHL hired him as a referee, and he took to the job with the same mischievous humour that had marked his career as a player. During one particular game he was being mercilessly heckled by a fan whom he knew to be a physician. At one point the fan yelled out, "Hey Clancy, you're makin' quite a few mistakes out there tonight!" Clancy shot back with, "Yeah, but at least I don't bury mine!"

Following his stint as an ice lawyer, Clancy returned to Maple Leaf Gardens where he put in long service as coach, assistant general manager,

and general dog's body. His role for many years might best be stated as the Leafs' ambassador of goodwill.

Clancy was a part of Maple Leaf Gardens for more than 50 years, and was still on the payroll the day he died, November 10, 1986. He was elected to the Hockey Hall of Fame in 1958.

Conn Smythe was the consummate scout. His keen eyes, so clearly seen here about 1932, were able to see past bad ice, poor coaching, and desperate equipment. He found many diamonds in the rough and polished them in farm teams across the continent before adding them to his prize collection, the Toronto Maple Leafs.

Imperial Oil Turofsky Collection, HHF

When the Leafs skated out for the 1930–31 campaign, they ushered in a new era of hockey in Toronto. For the next fifteen seasons the team would never miss post-season play. Clancy made an immediate impact on the team; the Leafs opened the season with five consecutive shutouts, and the crowds turned out in huge numbers to see the diminutive Irishman. Although the Leafs would not drink Stanley Cup champagne that year, the fans knew it was only a matter of time.

As the team grew in popularity, Smythe began to imagine a new kind of hockey facility, one with many more seats and a lot more class than the current Mutual Street Arena. During the early months of 1931 when hockey fans tuned their radios to Leaf games they heard Foster Hewitt promoting a new home for the Toronto Maple Leafs. He asked the fans to send in ten cents for which they would receive a souvenir of Conn Smythe's new Maple Leaf Gardens. No mere rink, the new ice palace would be the sort of place where folks could dress up in their finery and see high-class hockey. It was not to be a cold, smoke-filled hall for rink rats and slouches, but a sort of theatre, where husband and wife could spend a night out on the town.

Hockey fans responded in huge numbers; dimes poured into Smythe's office at a furious pace. The souvenir offer was a fund-raising scheme, of course, but it had a more immediate purpose. When Smythe had taken his ideas to investors in the business community, they at first dismissed the idea of regularly filling a huge hockey rink night after night during those depression days. But the flow of dimes from the public served as a market survey to convince Ed and Jack Bickell — as well as several other prominent businessmen — that Smythe's scheme merited closer consideration. Maple Leaf Gardens Ltd. was incorporated in February 1931 with Jack Bickell as its first president.

Smythe, Selke, and even Ace Bailey hit the bricks in a campaign to raise the big dollars needed to build the Gardens. Big investors were attracted, notably Sun Life Assurance of Montreal, which provided $500,000. But the Gardens could not have been built (not just then, at any rate) without strong public support. A $200,000 shortfall in financing was made up by members of various unions who were persuaded by Frank Selke to accept Gardens stock as part of their wages so that the project could go forth.

The new home of the Toronto Maple Leafs was to occupy land owned by the Eaton family, at the corner of Church and Carlton. Ed Bickell was so formidable in his bid for the property that the Eatons not only sold the land but gave a $35,000 option — 10 per cent of the purchase price — on shares in the new complex.

All the pieces of the puzzle were in place, and the first sod was turned on June 1, 1931. Smythe marshalled all of his leadership skills in keeping the project moving, and on November 12, 1931, just five months later, the Toronto Maple Leafs hosted the Chicago Blackhawks in the first game played at Maple Leaf Gardens. The Leafs lost 2–1.

Foster Hewitt, seen here in 1923, was a Leaf fan through and through. He began chirping the play-by-play on radio in March 1923 and in 1931 took his place in the gondola high above the action at Maple Leaf Gardens. Hewitt was a delight to radio and television audiences for more than 60 years and is the only broadcaster to have been inducted into the Hockey Hall of Fame.
HHF Archival Collection

Toronto Maple Leafs, 1932. In 1932 the Leafs won the Stanley Cup for the first time. It was the fourth time a team had won for Toronto.
Imperial Oil Turofsky Collection, HHF

These four "Ice Kings" hockey cards were issued to celebrate the 1932 Stanley Cup winners. They are among the first cards distributed by a chewing-gum company, the World Wide Gum Co. Ltd of Montreal.

Hayes Collection, HHF

In the previous season, Smythe had handed over the coaching reins to Art Duncan, freeing himself to concentrate on the Gardens project and scout new talent. He snapped up Alex Levinsky and Bob Gracie, and added Frank Finnigan and Harold Darragh before the start of the 1931–32 season. When the Leafs failed to win in their first five games, Smythe replaced Art Duncan with Dick Irvin, who had just been fired from the Chicago Blackhawks.

Irvin had seen play in several leagues and had coached the Blackhawks to the finals the previous season. He made his debut with the Leafs on November 28, 1931, and after defeating the Boston Bruins 6–5, the Leafs never looked back. Jackson, Primeau, and Conacher finished the season first, second, and fourth in scoring, and Lorne Chabot was a standout throughout the year.

On March 15 against Boston, Chabot caught the attention of the referee for tripping and was sent off to cool his heels in the penalty box. In those days, the goaltenders served their own penalties, so Horner, Levinsky, and Clancy all filled in for Chabot on occasion. They proved much better at stopping attackers than pucks — they all turn up in the goaltending register as having allowed one goal each in their brief careers in the net.

The Leafs cruised into post-season play after finishing second and beat out Chicago 6 goals to 2 in the first round. They had a tougher time against the Montreal Maroons and needed Bob Gracie's goal near the end of the first overtime period to secure a place in the Stanley Cup final.

➤

This 1933 action photograph from Maple Leaf Gardens shows the Leafs in full tilt against the New York Americans. New York goaltender Roy Worters is caught out of position by Toronto forwards Harvey Jackson, Charlie Conacher (9), and Buzz Boll (17), while future NHL president Red Dutton looks for the puck.

Imperial Oil Turofsky Collection, HHF

Clarence "Hap" Day was signed for the St. Pats in 1924 while still a student of pharmacy at the University of Toronto. Conn Smythe originally wanted Day to join his Varsity Grads team, but Hap decided that if he were going to play hockey, he might as well be paid for it. Tommy Gaston remembers that when the Gardens opened, Hap Day ran a small drugstore in the lobby.
Imperial Oil Turofsky Collection, HHF

Red Horner, ca. 1937. "Red Horner was more or less a body-checker. He liked to hit and he could certainly take his man out along the boards or on the blueline. When we played in those early days, we didn't shoot the puck in. We tried to carry it by the defenceman, so it gave him the opportunity to use his body. Horner was a pretty good puckhandler and he always gave his utmost." — Bob Davidson
Imperial Oil Turofsky Collection, HHF

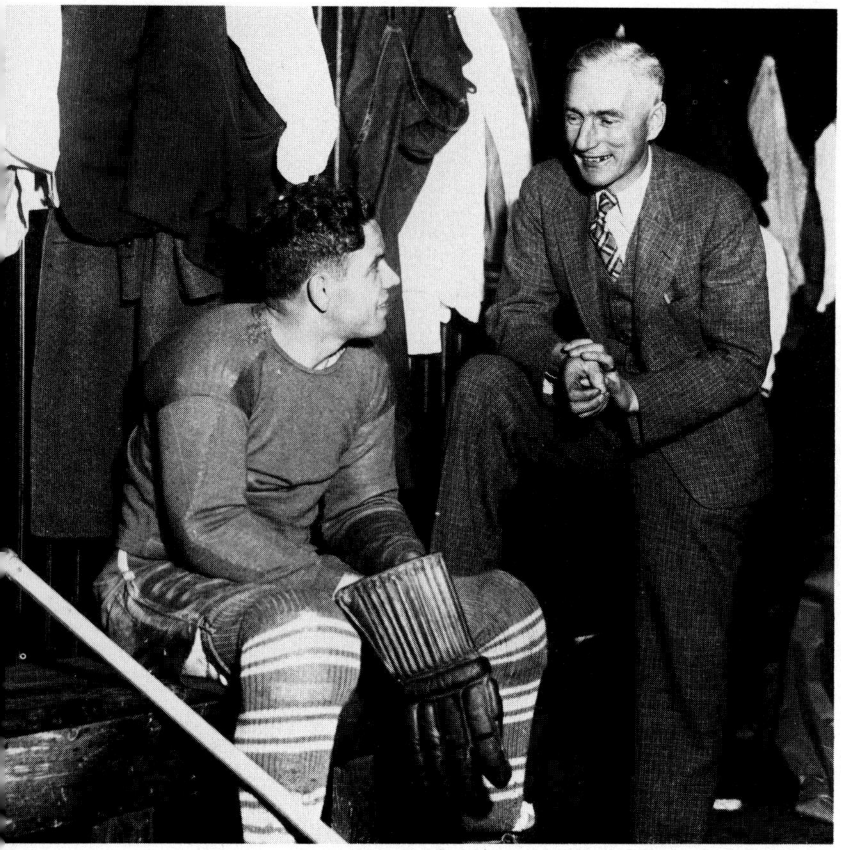

A young Red Horner takes advice from the great Dick Irvin, 1932. Irvin had seen plenty of action as a player in several leagues.

Imperial Oil Turofsky Collection, HHF

Red Horner played his entire professional career with the Leafs. He joined the team in 1927 at age 19 and never looked back. With PIMs of 167, 144, and 146, he wouldn't rank with today's sin-bin heroes, but from 1932 until his retirement in 1940, Horner led the league in penalties.

Imperial Oil Turofsky Collection, HHF

Ken Doraty is best remembered for one game and one goal. On the night of April 3, 1933, the Leafs and the Boston Bruins were battling through six periods of overtime when Coach Dick Irvin sent Doraty over the boards. Andy Blair pounced on a loose puck and threw it across to Doraty who scored to end the game at the 4:46 mark of the sixth overtime period. Doraty should also be remembered for another achievement: on January 16, 1934, the Leafs and Ottawa were tied 4–4 going into a 10-minute period of overtime. Doraty scored a "pure" hat trick to give the Leafs a 7–4 win. He is the only man ever to have scored three goals in one overtime period. The 10-minute regular-season overtime period, introduced in 1928, was discontinued in November 1941 because of wartime restrictions on train scheduling: the trains could no longer be delayed for the sake of a hockey game.

Imperial Oil Turofsky Collection, HHF

Once there, the Leafs did not waste their opportunity, scoring six goals in every match and winning the Cup in three straight games against the New York Rangers. The 1932 playoffs gave Dick Irvin his revenge against the Blackhawks, evened Smythe's score with the Rangers, and brought the Toronto Maple Leafs their first Stanley Cup.

The Leafs were an entertainment spectacle; there was rarely an empty seat at the Gardens, for the team was the best Toronto had ever known. The 1932–33 season saw the Leafs finish at the top of the NHL standings, with 24 wins in 48 games. Bill Thoms was a new face on the ice that year, as was Ken Doraty, who was signed from the Memorial

Alexandra Studios, the official photographers of the Toronto Maple Leafs in the thirties, produced this famous composite to announce the rolling stock of the 1933–34 Leaf squad.

Imperial Oil Turofsky Collection, HHF

Goalie George Hainsworth joined the Leafs in 1933–34. Conn Smythe had traded Lorne Chabot to get him, and Hainsworth responded by leading the league in victories in his first two seasons as a Maple Leaf. Here he battles the lowly Ottawa Senators as Albert LeDuc is stifled at the crease.

Imperial Oil Turofsky Collection, HHF

Cup winning Regina Pats. During the regular season, Doraty scored only five goals, but proved himself with his clutch play in the post-season.

The Leafs met the Boston Bruins in the first round of the 1933 playoffs, and with the series tied at two games each, the fifth and deciding match was played in Toronto on April 3. The Maple Leafs were decimated by injuries and dressed only 14 players, including the goaltender. At the end of regulation time, the game was scoreless, and it continued this way through five overtime periods. After the fifth overtime period, league and team officials met to decide some other way of ending the marathon game without a draw, but they could agree on nothing except another period of play. Smythe kept them talking as long as possible in order to give his boys a rest. Then he fired the team up by telling them that the officials were ready to call it a draw. Imagine their reaction, having just played eight periods of hockey to end up with a tie! They went back out on the ice, and at the 104-minute overtime mark Ken Doraty swooped in on Boston goaltender Tiny Thompson, sending the Leafs to the Stanley Cup finals.

The Leafs had no time to celebrate: they were required to play the first game of the finals later that very night — in New York City! The Rangers feasted on the band of overworked and injured Leafs, taking the series in four games. It had been a race well run, but the Cup eluded the Leafs, a trend that would continue for the balance of Dick Irvin's tenure as coach of the Toronto Maple Leafs.

February 14, 1934, Ace Bailey benefit game. Bailey recalls the game that ended his career two months earlier: "Dick Irvin was the coach and we were two men shy. Dick put me on the ice to kill the penalty with Horner and Clancy. Shore was coming down with the puck and I bothered him to centre ice. Then I swung over to my wing and took my man. Horner hit Shore and put him into the boards. Red picked up the puck and goes down to the Boston zone. I swung around Clancy and took up Horner's position. They (Boston) came again with the puck. On their way out, Mr. Shore knocked my feet from underneath me. My head hit first and it fractured both sides. I was unconscious for 15 days.

"The boys told me what happened. Shore was over at the other side of the arena. Red went over and said, "Put up your hands — I'm gonna hit ya." Shore didn't put his hands up and POW! Red really hit him. It took six men to take him off." — Ace Bailey

Imperial Oil Turofsky Collection, HHF

Over the next seven seasons, the Leafs made the Stanley Cup finals five times, but not until 1942 would they finally taste Stanley Cup victory. As the thirties rolled by, the Leafs saw some of their best talent lose the competitive advantage of youth.

The Kid Line of Harvey Jackson, Joe Primeau, and Charlie Conacher played their best hockey during this period. Year after year they were at the top of the NHL scoring ladder, but injuries and age caught up with them by the end of the decade. Joe Primeau retired at the conclusion of the 1935–36 season. Charlie Conacher battled numerous injuries and illnesses and was eventually sold to Detroit for the 1938–39 campaign. Busher Jackson was traded to the New York Americans for Sweeney Schriner, and by the end of the decade, the Kid Line was a memory. Though the Gardens faithful may have rebelled at seeing the last of the "Kids," Sweeney Schriner was no small compensation.

The Leafs lost one of their more colourful and steady goal scorers on December 12, 1933, when Ace Bailey was struck down from behind by Eddie Shore of Boston. Bailey survived two operations and one obituary in a Boston newspaper, but his career was over. The spirit of the 1932 Leafs, King Clancy skated his last game on November 23, 1936. The biggest single-player deal in the history of the game continued to pay off for years to come however, as Clancy did long and loyal service for the organization until his death in 1986.

Ace Bailey (right) and Eddie Shore before the start of the first NHL All-Star game.

Imperial Oil Turofsky Collection

The NHL organized its first all-star game on February 14, 1934, as a benefit for Ace Bailey, the sharp shooter who was cut down in a duel with the Boston Bruins in December of 1933. Bailey survived, but his playing days were over. The Leafs challenged an all-star team assembled from the rest of the NHL. The game was a huge draw, not just because Bailey was well loved in Toronto, but also because the best players in professional hockey had come together as a unit to play the Maple Leafs. When the cheering was over, the Leafs had defeated the herculean team 6–2.

Imperial Oil Turofsky Collection, HHF

Ace Bailey drops the puck for the ceremonial faceoff to begin the all-star game held in his honour, February 14, 1934. The men to take the face are Montreal's Howie Morenz for the All-Stars, and Joe Primeau for the "Aces."

Imperial Oil Turofsky Collection, HHF

"I had laid a couple of charges, one against Shore and one against the Boston club. Dr. Russ called me up and said they would like to see me. I met Dr. Russ and he said, 'Lookit, they want you to withdraw those charges, and if you do they'll put on a benefit game for you. Heck, if you have your case in Boston, you might be lucky if you get $5000.' Smythe and the gang agreed and I agreed to withdraw the charges and so we put on that benefit game. That gate was worth $20,000. They gave the money to a trust company and they handled it for me."
— Ace Bailey

Imperial Oil Turofsky Collection, HHF

The Jackson brothers, Art and Harvey ("Busher"), pose for the cameras at Maple Leaf Gardens in 1934. Art Jackson played with the Leafs from 1934 to 1937, returning in 1945 to earn his only Stanley Cup ring. Harvey received his nickname by disobeying the orders of long-time Leaf trainer, Tim Daly. Jackson was sitting out a match in his rookie year because of an injury, and Daly asked him to carry some sticks to the bench. Jackson refused, saying, "I ain't here to carry sticks, I'm here to play hockey." Daly replied, "Kid, you're nothing but a fresh busher" (meaning a backwoods bush-leaguer).
Imperial Oil Turofsky Collection, HHF

Centreman for the most famous of Maple Leaf trios, the "Kid Line," Joe Primeau made his debut with the team in 1928. He slumped during his first season, but in 1929 Conn Smythe put him on a line with Conacher and Jackson, and the Kid Line was born. "Gentleman" Joe retired from the team in 1936, but he kept his hand in the game as a coach. He became the first — and perhaps the only — coach to win the "Triple Crown of Hockey." He coached winners to the Memorial Cup and the Allan Cup, and in April of 1951 he led the Toronto Maple Leafs to the Stanley Cup.
Imperial Oil Turofsky Collection, HHF

The retirement of his best players came as no surprise to Conn Smythe, and he continually worked to maintain a high-calibre team. He replenished the stock by supporting farm clubs all over Canada and the U.S. in exchange for tips on hot young prospects. And he didn't limit his scouting to hockey rinks, for it was not just great hockey players he was after, but rather great athletes. While Squib Walker scouted the western sporting venues, Smythe followed the lacrosse circuits and the football loops in his search for the kind of grace and timing that he knew made great hockey players. When he found Syl Apps playing football for McMaster University in Hamilton, he put Apps on the Leaf negotiation list without even asking whether the kid could play hockey. Apps wasn't only an adept footballer, Smythe had to wait until after the 1936 Olympics where Apps represented Canada, finishing sixth, in the pole-vaulting event.

Conn Smythe and Coach Hap Day have good reason to relax: during these days of the "Gashouse Gang," winning hockey games was just par for the course.
Imperial Oil Turofsky Collection, HHF

Francis Michael "King" Clancy, 1932. "Clancy —there was a good leader. He didn't give a damn how big the other guy was, Clancy would go for him." — Ace Bailey

Imperial Oil Turofsky Collection, HHF

Gordie Drillon

Gordie Drillon was discovered by Smythe's scouting army in New Brunswick, and was sent off to a farm club in Syracuse, New York. In 1937, when the "Big Bomber," Charlie Conacher, was off his game and Smythe needed another big front liner to fill the gap, he turned to Gordie Drillon.

As a rookie, Drillon performed adequately on a line with Syl Apps and Busher Jackson, but his second year was spectacular. He scored 52 points in 1938, an even split between goals and assists, and he led the league in points. In that same year he won the Lady Byng Trophy and an all-star appointment.

Drillon never slumped, but he never again achieved the excellence that he had in 1938. He figured prominently in the lineup for the balance of his career, but was frustrated in his quest for the Stanley Cup. In 1942 it looked as if Drillon would get his silver ring: he'd been appointed an all-star for the third time, and the Leafs were winning big. In the finals against Detroit, Drillon had been unable to score, and the Leafs lost the first three games. In the scramble to turn the situation around, both Drillon and Bucko McDonald were benched in favour of Don Metz and Hank Goldup. It was a bitter-sweet victory for Drillon as he sat by and watched his teammates make one of the greatest comebacks in hockey history — they went on to defeat the Red Wings in four straight.

In 1942 Drillon was dealt to Montreal to play his final year of professional hockey and rack up an impressive 50 points in 50 games. The last Maple Leaf to win the scoring championship, in 1975 Drillon became the first Maritimer to be inducted into the Hockey Hall of Fame.

Conn Smythe signed a number of players who made their names on the lacrosse fields, but one who escaped his grasp was Bucko McDonald (far left). Smythe made it known, through a rare slip of the tongue to his rival Jack Adams, that he had spotted a great-looking athlete playing lacrosse. The sly Adams got McDonald's signature on the dotted line first. McDonald was eventually traded to Toronto in 1938 and played both professional hockey and lacrosse in Maple Leaf Gardens.

Imperial Oil Turofsky Collection, HHF

Flash Hollett first made his name playing lacrosse. Again it was the easy way and athletic sense that attracted Smythe to this future star; he had no idea whether Hollett could play ice hockey.

The 1934–35 and 1935–36 seasons saw the Leafs reach the finals again, only to be turned back by the Montreal Maroons and the Detroit Red Wings, respectively. Charlie Conacher proved not only that he could put the puck in the net but, on March 16, 1935, that he could stop it as well. He replaced injured goalie George Hainsworth and stopped everything thrown his way.

The Leafs had a very rough winter in 1936–37 but the year was not without consolation. The nucleus of the team that would win big in the 1940s came together that year. Syl Apps, Turk Broda, and Gordie Drillon all wore the Maple Leaf for the first time that season. The 1938–39 Leafs boasted 10 players who had been added since 1935–36 — an unusually large number of new faces for the times. Included on this squad were Bingo Kampman, Murph Chamberlain, Gus Marker, and another big man on the lacrosse field, Bucko McDonald.

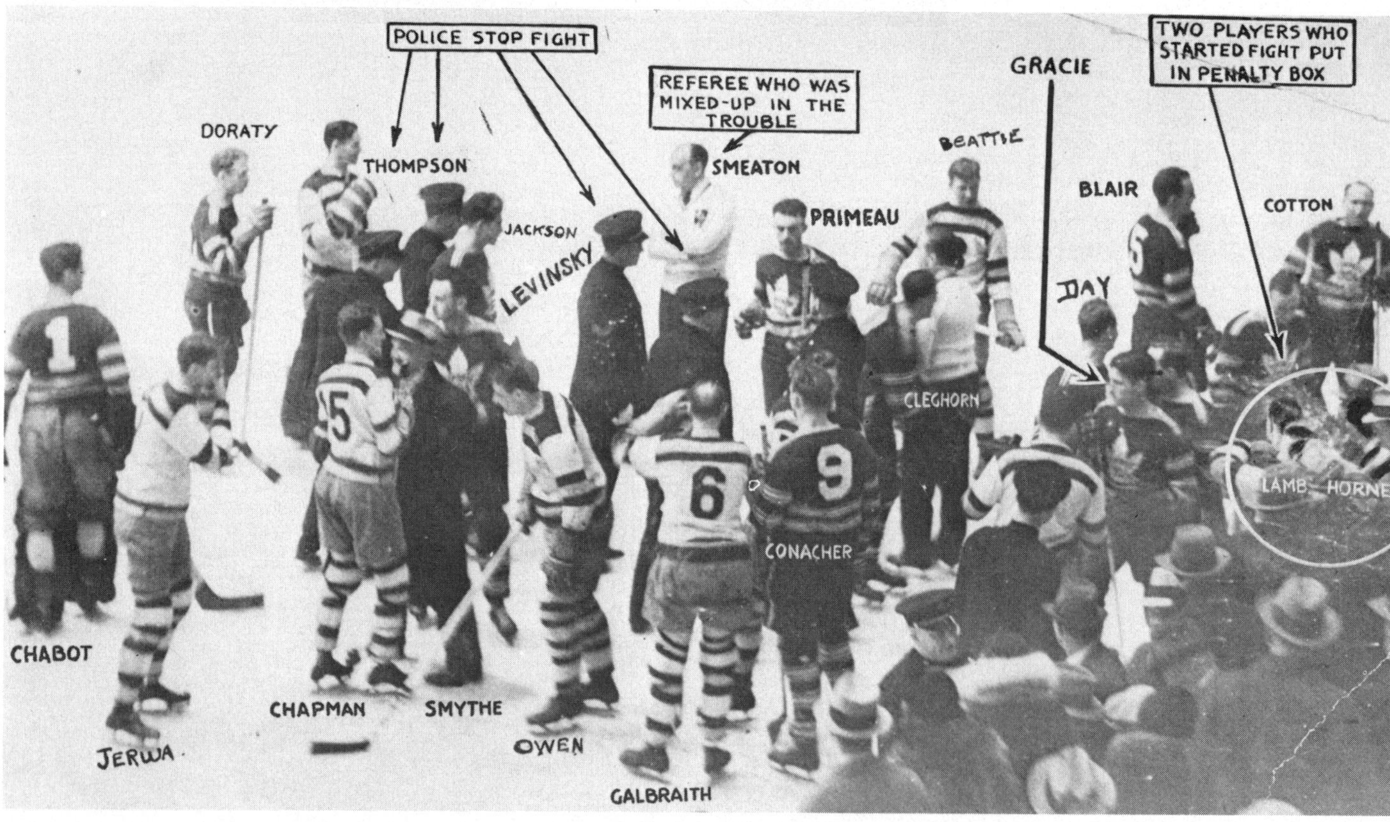

Conn Smythe joins his troops in the "alley" to help settle a few matters in this 1933 game against Boston. On a subsequent occasion, March 12, 1936, Smythe got into an argument with Canadiens playing coach Sylvio Mantha and, after a penalty call, joined Mantha in the cooler. Leafs coach Dick Irvin joined in by cuffing Mantha, starting a donnybrook of exceptional proportions. Soon, referee Mike Rodden and Montreal executive Ernie Savard leapt into the fray, and were joined moments later by league president Frank Calder.

Imperial Oil Turofsky Collection, HHF

Then as now, popular sports figures were sought after to endorse commercial products. This 1930s version of the Leafs had no compunction about posing for a pipe-manufacturer's advertisement.
HHF Archival Collection

Syl Apps

It is well known that Conn Smythe never limited himself to ice rinks in his never-ending search for new players. Many of his best prospects were discovered on the lacrosse pitch, the baseball diamond, or the football field. Not all this sporting talent made the transition to hockey successfully, but when Smythe discovered Olympic track star Syl Apps, he hit pay dirt.

Luckily for Smythe and the Leafs, Apps' prowess at pole-vaulting was matched by his abilities on the ice. The "gentle giant" joined the Leafs after the 1936 Olympics. He was an instant success, leading the NHL in assists and winning the first Calder Trophy. When team captain, Red Horner, retired in 1940, Apps was named as his replacement, a position he held with honour and respect until his own retirement in 1948.

With Apps as their spiritual leader in the dressing room and their offensive catalyst on the ice, the Leafs won three Stanley Cups. The squad was molded by his hand. The Leafs of the forties placed an emphasis on team performance, and Apps led the way with unselfish dedication to his teammates. He had only one personal ambition: he wanted to hit the 200-goal plateau, and he often insisted that he would retire after he reached that milestone.

In 1947–48, with one game left in the schedule, Apps was still two goals shy of his objective. As the Leafs faced Detroit on the last night of the season, Apps netted a hat trick to put himself over the 200-goal mark and reach career highs in both goals and points. With typical modesty, he dismissed his own performance, preferring to stress the team's first-place finish.

After the Leafs won the Cup that spring, Apps retired, content to bow out of the game while still at the height of his talents. The Leafs felt the loss of his wisdom and leadership for many years after. He was elected to the Hockey Hall of Fame in 1961.

Turk Broda, ca. 1938. Broda has been called the greatest money goaltender of all time. He played 14 NHL seasons — all for the Leafs — and made the playoffs 13 times, taking home Stanley Cup rings on five occasions. In his 102 post-season games, he registered 13 shutouts and a fantastic 1.98 goals-against average.
HHF Archival Collection

The 1939–40 squad featured a wide array of talent and tremendous bench strength. Sweeney Schriner had come from the Americans, and Bashing Billy Taylor had been brought in from the Oshawa Generals. "The Whirling Dervish," Wally Stanowski, whipped in from the St. Boniface Seals, and Hank Goldup rounded out the newcomers. Despite the new faces, the Leafs motored into the finals again but their luck was not to change. The New York Rangers won the finals in six nailbiters, three of them overtime matches.

Prior to the 1940–41 season, Dick Irvin asked permission to talk to the Canadiens about their vacant coaching position. Smythe agreed that the change might be good both for Irvin and for the Toronto Maple Leafs. Irvin had led the team to the finals seven times, including five of the last six years, but the team had come up short all five outings. Smythe was proven right on both counts: Irvin had a successful career with the Canadiens, winning three Cups, and no other coach appointed by Smythe would lose a Stanley Cup final. In the next 27 years, the Leafs would reach the finals 12 times,

Murph Chamberlain played with the Leafs from 1937 to 1940 and was known for his hard-nosed fore-checking.
Imperial Oil Turofsky Collection, HHF

Rudolph "Bingo" Kampman, whose nickname comes from the sound he made when he crashed an on-ice foe into the boards, was teamed with Red Horner on the blueline for much of his career, giving the Leafs the NHL's deadliest pair of body-bashers. Kampman played with the Leafs from 1937 to 1941, when he enlisted in the military.
Imperial Oil Turofsky Collection, HHF

Tradition has it that this 1934 shot was taken after Howie Morenz of the Habs put one of his patented moves on Red Horner, leaving him behind to reclaim a certain piece of equipment he had just been faked out of. King Clancy and Hap Day are on hand to give Horner moral support.
Imperial Oil Turofsky Collection, HHF

Toronto Maple Leafs, 1940–41.
Imperial Oil Turofsky Collection, HHF

These four men were all captains of the Toronto Maple Leafs (left to right): Bob Davidson, Syl Apps, Ted Kennedy, Hap Day.

Imperial Oil Turofsky Collection, HHF

and lose only twice: the losses are credited to Punch Imlach, a man whom Smythe did not sign. Irvin, during his coaching career, lost a total of 12 Stanley Cup finals, a National Hockey League record.

Hap Day took over from Irvin as Leaf coach in 1940 and guided the team to second place in his first campaign. Red Horner retired prior to the season, and without his aggressive play the Leafs actually played two consecutive penalty-free games. On March 16, 1941, the Leafs were witness to an innovation that would become *de rigueur* for teams needing a clutch goal. Chicago coach Paul Thompson pulled his goalie for the extra attacker, the first recorded use of this strategy in NHL history. Turk Broda won the Vezina Trophy while Gordie Drillon and Syl Apps finished third and fourth in the scoring race.

Frank Selke moved into the manager's office when Conn Smythe dusted off his battle fatigues for European service, and Selke prepared for a war of his own. He acquired Lorne Carr, Sweeney Schriner's old New York Americans linemate, and put them on a line with Billy Taylor. New talent, including Ernie Dickens and Bob Goldham who came up from the farm in Hershey, helped lead the Leafs to another second place finish.

The Leafs took out the Rangers in six games, and reached the finals for the first time with Hap Day behind the bench. The curse that had stifled the Leafs seemed still to have some power over them. They lost the first three games of the finals to Detroit by scores of 3–2, 4–2, and 5–2. The Red Wings would have the series in one more game.

"Day was the best coach I've ever seen in the NHL. He was a complete analyst of the game, who knew the game thoroughly. He was a very strict coach and insisted on a hundred per cent effort out on the ice. He had us play to a system that four times was successful in winning the Stanley Cup." — Ted Kennedy

Imperial Oil Turofsky Collection, HHF

Coach Hap Day (far right) pauses with a group of Leaf regulars and Leaf hopefuls after a 1941 practice with the American Hockey League's (AHL) Rhode Island (Providence) Reds. Although the Leafs did not have a farm agreement with the Reds, it was not unusual for the NHL and AHL teams to meet for practice and exhibition games both during the season and in training camp.
Imperial Oil Turofsky Collection, HHF

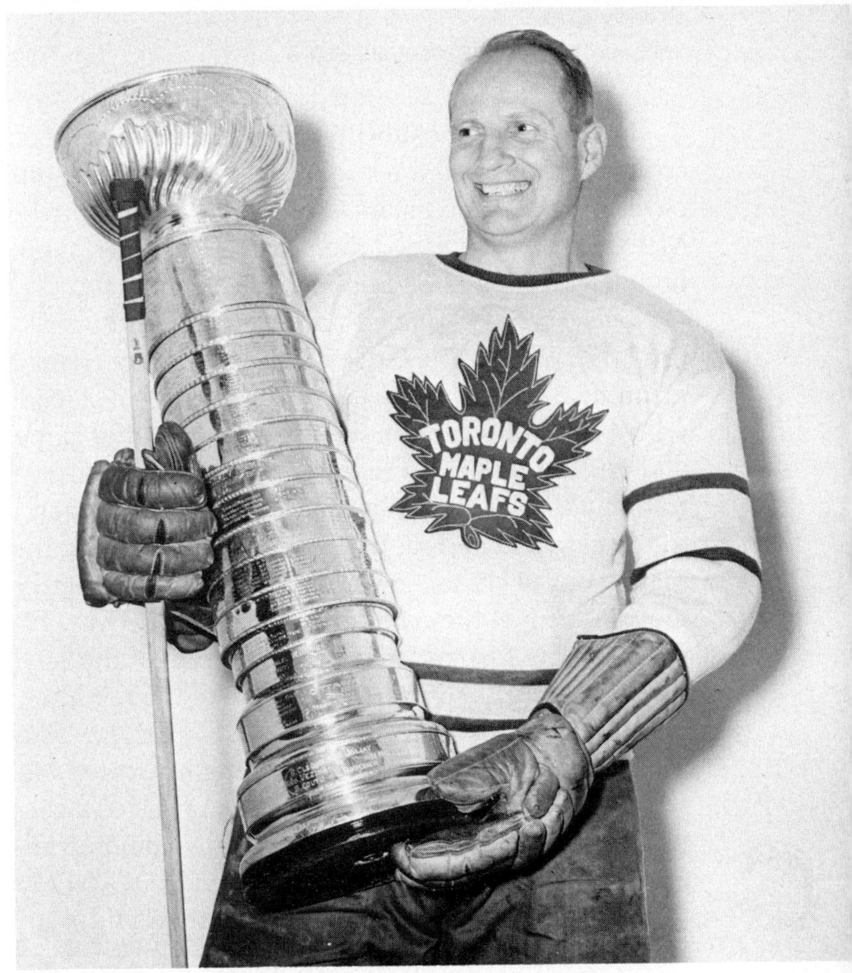

"When I played on the team, Hap Day was the captain and also the outstanding defenceman. He was a tremendous skater and puck carrier. I wouldn't say he was a great body-checker, but he could tie you up in front of the net. He had a great trick: he would stick his stick between the opponent's legs, then hang onto the other stick. The opposing player couldn't move. He got away with it numerous times. When he coached the Leafs, he taught our defencemen exactly what he did when he played defence." — Bob Davidson
Imperial Oil Turofsky Collection, HHF

The Toronto Maple Leafs, 1941–42. The 1941–42 Leafs are the only NHL team to have lost the first three games in a final round and then come back to win the Stanley Cup.

Imperial Oil Turofsky Collection, HHF

In one of the most brilliant yet controversial coaching moves on the books, Hap Day, for reasons of his own, benched stars Gordie Drillon and Bucko McDonald. He replaced them with Don Metz, who hadn't played a game in two weeks, and Ernie Dickens, who had played only 10 games in his entire NHL career. The Grosse Pointe regulars were grinning and cheering as the Wings held a 3–2 lead with 14 minutes remaining. Syl Apps tied the game and Nick Metz potted the go-ahead goal. The frustration at the Detroit Olympia was at a peak when the final bell sounded. Jack Adams, in a move completely out of character, raced out onto the ice and took a swing at the referee, Mel Harwood. Even with Adams suspended for the duration of the series, the Wings had to win only one of the remaining three games.

Day was not finished rearranging his roster. He sent in Gaye Stewart, a raw rookie, to replace three-year veteran Hank Goldup. Day's move paid off in game five as Don Metz scored a hat trick in a 9–3 thrashing, leaving the Red Wings startled and shaken.

Turk Broda forced a seventh game by shutting out the Wings 3–0 in game six. Conn Smythe was on the scene at Maple Leaf Gardens for that big seventh game, but he was not allowed into the dressing room, or anywhere near the players. It is not understood why or how the directors kept him at bay, but he respected their wishes — for a while. At the end of the second period, with the Leafs trailing 1–0 Smythe made his move. Sneaking past security guards, he entered the dressing room and spoke directly to the trio he knew could win this game and series. Schriner, Carr, and Taylor sat spellbound as The Major gave his orders. "What'cha worryin' about, boss," said Schriner, "We'll get ya a couple of goals!" They delivered. Taylor and Carr set up Schriner for two goals and Pete Langelle fired home the winner as the Leafs completed the most astounding comeback in sporting history. Never before or since has a team rebounded from a three-game deficit to recover and win a championship series. On that night, the Maple Leafs were presented with their second Stanley Cup, the fifth in the history of the city.

In the seventh game of the 1942 Stanley Cup final, with the series tied and the Leafs trailing Detroit 1–0 at the end of the second period, Billy Taylor and Lorne Carr set Sweeney Schriner up for two goals. Left to right: Murph Chamberlain, Taylor, Carr, Gordie Drillon, Schriner.

Imperial Oil Turofsky Collection, HHF

"Gordie Drillon was an excellent goal scorer. No other Leaf has led the league in scoring since he led it in 1937–38. He could put the puck in any way at all; he could put it in along the ice, he could beat a goaltender on a shift, he could throw it high. He wasn't a great back-checker, but as an offensive player he was one of the best." — Bob Davidson

HHF Archival Collection

April 5, 1942. Pete Langelle (Number 8) has just scored a historic goal in the seventh game of the Cup final at 9:43 of the third period. Langelle's marker, coming just after Schriner's first goal, gave the Leafs a 2–1 lead and proved to be the Cup-winning goal. Langelle's ecstatic teammates are Johnny McCreedy and Bob Goldham.

Imperial Oil Turofsky Collection, HHF

"Turk was a great goalkeeper, particularly a playoff goalkeeper. When the chips were really down and the Stanley Cup was on the line, Turk was as great as I've ever seen. He was a great athlete besides . . . an excellent ballplayer and a fine golfer." — Ted Kennedy

Imperial Oil Turofsky Collection, HHF

Conn Smythe and Hap Day go over a scouting report with Leafs' super-sleuth Squib Walker (far right). Walker was the Leafs' chief scout in western Canada during the forties, and most of the Leafs from the West were spotted by the Squib.

Imperial Oil Turofsky Collection, HHF

The next two seasons saw the Toronto roster nearly emptied of star material. Nick and Don Metz, Bingo Kampman, Ernie Dickens, Bob Goldham, Syl Apps, Turk Broda, Sweeney Schriner, Billy Taylor, and Wally Stanowski all joined the Canadian Armed Forces in Europe.

The Leafs finished third in 1943 and 1944, losing in the semi-finals both times. The years were productive in other ways, however. In 1943 the Leafs traded Frank Eddolls to Montreal to obtain the rights to a young player on the Port Colborne senior team, Ted Kennedy. Kennedy played only two games that season but returned to become the backbone of the franchise. Gaye Stewart and Gus Bodner won consecutive Calder Trophies, ensuring strong Leaf teams of the future. The Leafs set two NHL marks in these years which still stand. Gus Bodner scored a goal in his first 15 seconds on the ice, and the Leafs and Hawks played a scoreless, penalty-free game.

Ted "Teeder" Kennedy

During the war years, when most of the able-bodied men in North America were enlisted for military service, the National Hockey League scurried around for young players to fill the many empty hockey uniforms. One of the new Leaf recruits was a 5-foot-11, 180-pound centreman by the name of Ted Kennedy. He was asked to fill the very big boots of Syl Apps, and he performed so well in his first season as a regular that, when Apps returned, Kennedy remained.

Kennedy was teamed with Vic Lynn and Howie Meeker, and the trio was dubbed the Second Kid Line. The three of them performed with the strength, determination, and solidarity that characterized the team in the 1940s; the Leafs won five Stanley Cups in that decade and one in the 1950s.

A natural leader of men, and a very level-headed player, Kennedy scored 231 goals in his 14 regular seasons and 29 more in his 10 post-season outings. Kennedy's steady play and understated stardom made him one of the best-loved players of his time, and today, though not active in the hockey community, he is still remembered by thousands of Toronto fans.

Nineteen sixty-six was a banner year for the Leafs at the Hockey Hall of Fame. Ted Kennedy was inducted along with Joe Primeau, Babe Pratt, and Max Bentley, all one-time Maple Leafs.

During the 1940s, the Leafs had a full house of talent, and a Stanley Cup championship was often in the cards. Here, Coach Hap Day, Ted Kennedy, Don Metz, Garth Boesch, Bill Ezinicki, and Turk Broda enjoy a game of bridge.

Imperial Oil Turofsky Collection, HHF

Frank McCool

Of all the storybook heroes whose careers have been compiled in the NHL history books, there is none more special to Leaf fans than Frank "Ulcers" McCool. During the 1944–45 season, with Turk Broda overseas and the Leafs searching frantically for a goalie to replace him, McCool arrived in Toronto to rewrite the record books.

The Leafs signed McCool, who was excused from active duty in the service because of severe stomach troubles, out of the senior leagues in Calgary. Ulcers may have been a worry-wart, but he faced the NHL sharpshooters with ice-water in his veins. McCool appeared in all 50 games for the Leafs during the winter of 1944–45, leading the league in shutouts and winning the Calder Trophy. Despite these awards the jury was still out on McCool, waiting until the post-season to bring home their verdict.

In the semi-finals the Leafs faced the Montreal Canadiens, a firewagon group of snipers that had led the NHL in both offence and defence. *Les bleu-blanc-rouge* were not prepared for the stone wall the Leafs put between the pipes, and the tone of the series was set in game 1 when McCool shut out Montreal in a 1–0 nailbiter. The Leafs downed the Habs in six games and moved into the finals against Detroit, setting the stage for the most brilliant Stanley Cup performance by any goaltender.

Frank McCool became the ultimate Stanley Cup hero, shutting down the Red Wings in a fashion never seen before or since. Detroit couldn't score until the 8:35 mark of game 4, but by then McCool's place in hockey lore was secured. Detroit won games 4, 5 and 6, and then the Leafs took the Cup with a gutsy 2–1 victory in the decisive seventh game. McCool never played another Stanley Cup game, but his four playoff shutouts in only 13 games — the only four in his playoff career — earned him a special place in the history of the Toronto Maple Leafs.

Toronto Maple Leafs, 1944–45.
HHF Archival Collection

Nineteen forty-five was the year of Frank "Ulcers" McCool. McCool was an amateur goalie who had been brought in from Calgary for the season. He won the Calder Trophy, but his 3.22 average can only be considered mediocre. His playoff performance, however, showed him to be the stuff record books are made of.

With the outstanding play of Babe Pratt on defence, the Leafs finished third overall on the season and made another run at the Stanley Cup. They took Montreal in the semi-finals, and met their arch-rivals, the Detroit Red Wings, for the finals. McCool recorded three consecutive shutouts to open the series, an all-time record. The Wings came back with three straight wins of their own, two of them on Harry Lumley shutouts. With the score tied 1–1 late in the third period of game 7, Babe Pratt, the rushing badboy defenceman, slammed home a Nick Metz pass and the Leafs skated off with the Stanley Cup.

The Leafs battle the Wings during the semi-finals of 1947. Garth Boesch (centre) has decided to defend Turk Broda without the benefit of a stick, but no one can argue with the results: the Leafs won this game and the series.
Imperial Oil Turofsky Collection, HHF

TORONTO MAPLE LEAFS
BOSTON BRUINS
RANGERS
BLACK HAWKS
QUAKERS
PRICE 15¢
OFFICIAL PROGRAMME
MAPLE LEAF GARDENS
TORONTO
CANADA

Stanley Cup winning teams, 1931–1949
HHF Archival Collection

◄
This Maple Leaf Gardens program from the 1930s shows the flags of the NHL teams. This copy bears the signatures of many of the Leafs from the 1931–32 Stanley Cup winning team.
HHF Archival Collection

MAPLE LEAF GARDENS

"The Heart of a Nation's Sporting Life"

SCENES FROM THE 1942 STANLEY CUP TRIUMPH

P. Langelle, Major Smythe, M.C., D. Schriner, L. Carr

Conny Smythe congratulates Pete Langelle who scored the winning goal

Happy Day, Syl Apps, Major Smythe, M.C., N.H.L. President Frank Calder and Maple Leaf Gardens President G. R. Cottrelle

Mr. Calder presents hockey's most historic trophy

April 18th, 1942

Don Metz, Vice-Pres., Lieut-Col. W. A. H. MacBrien, Ernie Dickens, Vice-Pres., Major E. W. Bickle, V.D.

Hockey zealots of the executive and the two rookies who came through

Schriner ties the score one all and Canada's 'greatest ever' hockey crowd cheers him to the echo. 16,240 fans in the building and an estimated three million radio listeners sensed victory was near.

CAPT. SYL APPS

Hockey's finest competitor embraces the elusive Stanley Cup

Langelle scores the second goal literally blowing the roof off the Gardens as the cheers reverberate from Victoria to Sydney and the Arctics.

1942 *Maple Leaf Home Games Shown in Red*

DECEMBER

Maple Leaf Away Games Shown in Green 1942

SUN.	MON.	TUES.	WED.	THUR.	FRI.	SAT.
		ARMY vs. 1 NAVY	2	Maple Leafs at 3 CANADIENS	AIR FORCE vs. 4 RESEARCH	CANADIENS 5 TO-NIGHT
Maple Leafs at 6 DETROIT	7	ARMY vs. 8 AIR FORCE	9	CHICAGO 10 TO-NIGHT	RESEARCH vs. 11 NAVY	DETROIT 12 TO-NIGHT
Maple Leafs at 13 CHICAGO	ARMY vs. 14 RESEARCH	15	NAVY vs. 16 AIR FORCE	Maple Leafs at 17 CANADIENS	18	BOSTON 19 TO-NIGHT
Maple Leafs at 20 RANGERS	21	Maple Leafs at 22 RESEARCH vs. AIR FORCE BOSTON	23	24	(Christmas Day) 25 NAVY vs. ARMY	BOSTON 26 TO-NIGHT
Maple Leafs at 27 RANGERS	28	AIR FORCE vs. 29 NAVY	30	31		

Turk Broda, Bill Barilko, and Teeder Kennedy combine to remove Chicago Blackhawks' star Bill Mosienko from the Leaf crease, while Garth Boesch (far left), Roy Conacher, and Howie Meeker (far right) look on.
Imperial Oil Turofsky Collection, HHF

The following year the Leafs set another record: they were the first NHL team to win the Cup one year, and not make the playoffs the next. Aside from Gaye Stewart's league-leading 37 goals, it was a dismal year all round at Maple Leaf Gardens. Frank McCool played well below his ability and was released, Ted Kennedy was injured and missed most of the season, and veterans Sweeney Schriner and Lorne Carr both retired. Babe Pratt had problems of his own. The darling of the city, and one of the most loved players in the game, he innocently admitted to betting on his own performances. This did not sit well with league officials, who suspended him for life. But he successfully appealed and was back in action after missing only 16 games.

◄
Maple Leaf Gardens calendar, December, 1942.
HHF Archival Collection

"Mr. Smythe was the generalissimo of Maple Leaf Gardens, and I believe when this photo was taken he was general manager of the team. There isn't any question in my mind that he was the most influential person towards the success of the team. He was a great inspiration and a very tough boss, but I always felt he was a very fair boss as long as you were trying hard; that was all that he requested. We were all very fortunate to have played under his management." — Ted Kennedy
Imperial Oil Turofsky Collection, HHF

MAPLE LEAF GARDENS

JACK FOX
Princess Pats
The first pro hockey player to make the supreme sacrifice in the present war

MAJOR
E. W. BICKLE, V.D.
President

LIEUT.-COL.
W. A. H. MacBRIEN
Vice-Pres.

MAJOR
CONN SMYTHE, M.C.
on leave
O.C., 30th L.A.A. BATTERY, R.C.A-A

TORONTO MAPLE LEAFS

THE
GARDENS EXECUTIVE

Players on Active Service
and
1944 Special Trophy Winners

J. P. BICKELL
Chairman of the Board

G. R. COTTRELLE
O.B.E.

J. Y., MURDOCH, K.C.
Vice-Pres.

LIEUT.-COL.
BARKER
V.C., D.F.C., M.C.
(Deceased)
Our First President

PO
JOHNNY McCREEDY
R.C.A.F.

O.S.
JOE KLUKAY
R.C.N.V.R.

PTE.
JACK INGOLDSBY
Army

LIEUT.
NICK KNOTT
Army

PTE.
BUCK JONES
Army

BDR.
BINGO KAMPMAN
Army

PO
ERNIE DICKENS
R.C.A.F.

PTE.
BILLIE TAYLOR
Army

LIEUT.
A. "LEX" CHISHOLM
Army

O.S.
BOB GOLDHAM
R.C.N.V.R.

PTE.
JACK FORSEY
Army

SGT.
WALLY STANOWSKI
R.C.A.F.

O.S.
JACKIE HAMILTON
R.C.N.V.R.

CAPT.
BOBBY COPP
Army

AC2
DON METZ
R.C.A.F.

CPL.
BUDDY HELLYER
R.C.A.F.

O.S.
D. "RED" GARRETT
R.C.N.V.R.

LIEUT.
GAYE STEWART
R.C.N.V.R.

PTE.
VICTOR GRIGG
Army

PO
SHEP. MAYER
R.C.A.F.

PTE.
BUDDY POILE
Army

PTE.
ALBERT "RED" TILSON
Army

Hockey's Most Sensational Upset. George Boothman scores go ' No. 2 in the opening game of the 1944 Stanley Cup Series, won by Toronto Maple Leafs at Montreal Forum on arch 21st. The first and only loss for the powerful Champion Montreal Canadiens on home ice in twenty-five scheduled and five playoff games. Morris and Boothman scored for Toronto in the first period—J. Hamilton in the second—Toe Blake scored Canadiens' lone goal in third period.

LOOK UNDER THE PAD FOR NATIONAL HOCKEY LEAGUE SCHEDULE

1945 SEPTEMBER 1945

SUN	MON	TUE	WED	THU	FRI	SAT
						1
2	3	4	5	6	7	8
9	10	11	12	13	14	15
16	17	18	19	20	21	22
23/30	24	25	26	27	28	29

WALTER "BABE" PRATT
1944 All Star Defence
Toronto's First Winner
Dr. David A. Hart Trophy
Most Valuable Player Award

LIEUT.
TOMMY ANDERSON

SGT.
RHYS THOMSON
Army

LAC
PETE LANGELLE

L/CPL.
SYL APPS
Army

PTE.
NICK METZ
Army

SGT.
"BAZ" BASTIEN
Army

PTE.
KEN DIXON

PTE.
TURK BRODA
Army

GUS BODNAR
1944 Winner
Frank Calder Trophy
Best Rookie Award

Maple Leaf Gardens program, March 8, 1947, featuring Gaye Stewart on the cover. Stewart won the Calder Trophy in 1943 and was the last Leaf to lead the NHL in goals scored when he fired home 37 pucks in 1945.

HHF Archival Collection

◄

Toronto Maple Leafs 1945 calendar depicting members of the team who served in the armed forces.

HHF Archival Collection

In Toronto Babe Pratt (second from left) found his kind of people; his ranging defensive style made him a welcome and popular addition to the rink, and among his mates. Here, Pratt seems to be enjoying the spoils of victory.
Imperial Oil Turofsky Collection, HHF

A rare moment when Conn Smythe was on the outside looking in. The fencing itself is worth noting. In the days of wire mesh fan protection, it would have been far more difficult to rattle the puck around the "glass." There was no "shoot and scoot" hockey in those days.
Imperial Oil Turofsky Collection, HHF

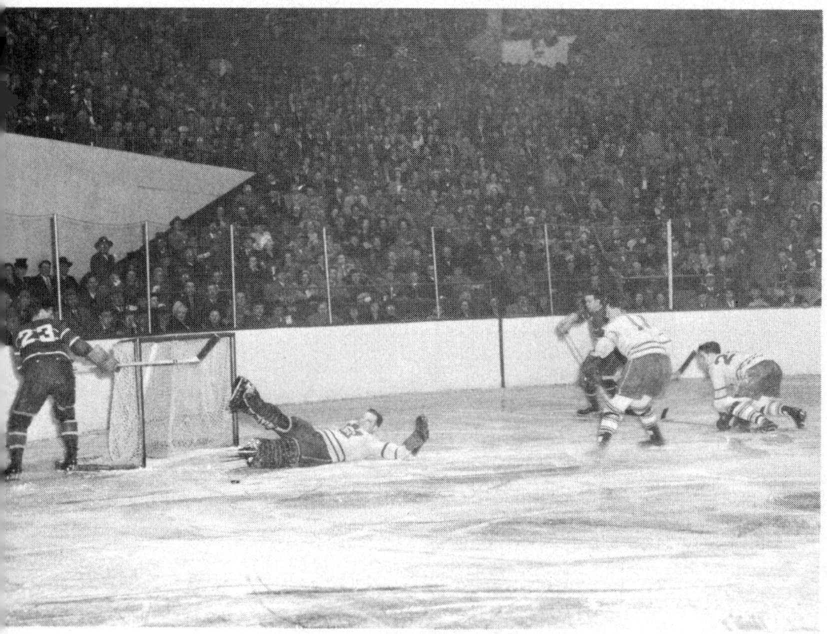

Turk Broda sprawls to rob Montreal Canadiens' forward Murdo McKay's (Number 23) attempt to score his first NHL goal, 1947. Broda had numerous challenges to his throne but always seemed to hold off the threatened coup. In the 1939–40 season, Broda was slumping, so Smythe gave Phil Stein a chance between the pipes. Stein, a long-time back-up who had never actually played before, held the Bruins to a 2–2 overtime tie in his first game. He got the next start as well, but took a shot off the chin in the pre-game warm-up. Broda returned, won the game, and went on to capture the Vezina Trophy that year. Stein never played another NHL game.
Imperial Oil Turofsky Collection, HHF

In another development, Frank Selke followed Dick Irvin into the Montreal Canadiens camp. There are several conflicting stories as to why Selke left the Leafs. Some say that it was a power play between Selke, Smythe, and president Jack Bickell. Others say it was Selke's insubordination to Smythe. In any case, Frank Selke took enormous hockey skills with him to the Montreal Forum. With Selke out of the picture, Smythe consolidated his power at the Gardens. There was undoubtedly a power struggle with Jack Bickell and other large shareholders of the Maple Leaf empire. Smythe emerged victorious with 30 per cent ownership — and the presidency — of Maple Leaf Gardens Ltd. and settled into a period of resounding success. His player changes came fast and furious and brought Toronto consecutive Stanley Cups in 1947, 1948, and 1949.

Fleming "Mac" MacKell wearing the uniform of the Pittsburgh Hornets in 1947. MacKell spent parts of five seasons (1947–1952) with the Leafs before carving out a fine career in Boston. The Pittsburgh Hornets were the Leafs' main professional farm team, and the threat of demotion to the Steel City usually brought out the best in players. The City of Pittsburgh decided to close down its rink in 1956, leaving the Hornets without a home and the Leafs without a farm team.

Fitzsimmons Collection, HHF

Babe Pratt

Conn Smythe considered Babe Pratt to be the Leafs' "all time all-star." He is the only man to end up in the Hockey Hall of Fame (1966) after having been banished from NHL play.

Pratt came up through the New York Rangers farm system and was chosen by Rangers manager Lester Patrick to replace Ching Johnson. But try as he might, Patrick could not control Pratt's antics on or off the ice, so he sent Babe north to Conn Smythe's Toronto Maple Leafs. Smythe was more Pratt's kind of man: he appreciated cards and ponies and was understanding of human ambitions and frailties. Pratt, with the reins loosened, blossomed into one of the most celebrated rushing defencemen of all time. In 1943–44 he won the coveted Hart Trophy, setting a defenceman's record with 57 points in the season — a record that stood for 21 years.

While Pratt was with the Leafs — and perhaps tutored by Smythe off the ice as well as on — his career was temporarily clouded by scandal. Following a serious accusation, league president Red Dutton summoned Pratt and asked him if he'd been dealing with gamblers. Pratt freely admitted that he had placed money on the Leafs to win. He was banished from further NHL play, with the proviso that the matter would be reviewed by the league's board of governors. The governors considered his plea for mercy, took a vote, and Pratt was back on Maple Leaf Gardens ice a scant couple of weeks after his "lifetime banishment" was decreed.

With the scandal behind him, Pratt continued to make a career in the rinks he loved. His Hall of Fame biography toasts him as a player, a coach, and finally as a goodwill ambassador with the Vancouver Canucks. For years Pratt was a fixture in the Vancouver press box. Before, during, and after the games, he would "hold court," regaling the Vancouver scribes with stories and jokes and an incisive analysis of the game in progress. On December 16, 1988, at the end of the second period of a Canucks–Flames battle, the Babe passed into legend, where he laughs and skates with the best who ever lived.

Winners of the Stanley Cup, 1947–48 Front row: Wally Stanowski, Teeder Kennedy, Conn Smythe, Syl Apps, Hap Day, W. A. H. MacBrien, Nick Metz. Middle row: Archie Campbell, Les Costello, Bill Ezinicki, Harry Watson, Turk Broda, Max Bentley, Vic Lynn, Howie Meeker, Tim Daly. Back row: Phil Sammis, Sid Smith, Bill Barilko, Garth Boesch, Jimmy Thomson, Gus Mortson, Joe Klukay.
Source unknown

Frank Selke (right) points out to Syl Apps the shaft he received from the Leafs. Selke resigned following the 1946 season, and went to Montreal to rebuild the Habs. Selke maintained that he was forced out by Smythe after disobeying the Major's orders by trading Frank Eddolls to the Canadiens for an unknown named Ted Kennedy. Smythe claimed that Selke was caught in a power play between Smythe and the Gardens' board of directors. When Selke left Smythe became president of the Leafs.
Imperial Oil Turofsky Collection, HHF

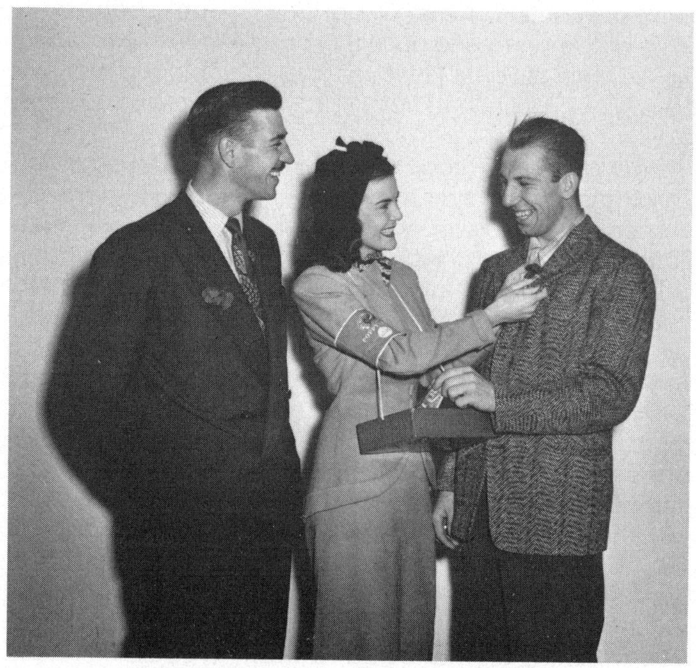

Remembrance Day, 1948. Garth Boesch and Max Bentley pose with a poppy seller. The Leafs have a tradition of making themselves available for the promotion of charity work and of setting an example for their fans.
Imperial Oil Turofsky Collection, HHF

Chicago goalie "Sugar" Jim Henry stretches to reach the flying disc as fellow Hawk Bob Goldham comes to his rescue. Off to the side (far left), the Bentley brothers, Max and Doug, fight for position. The 1947 trade that sent Max Bentley to the Leafs was one of the biggest swaps in NHL history and paid off handsomely for the Leafs — in the short term at least. Max and Doug, teammates for years with the Hawks before the swap, finished their playing days reunited as members of the New York Rangers.

Imperial Oil Turofsky Collection, HHF

In 1946–47, the squad featured 12 men who were not on the Cup winner of 1945. Among the new faces were Garth Boesch, Howie Meeker, Vic Lynn, Gus Mortson, Harry Watson, Joe Klukay, and Bill Barilko. The Leafs finished second overall and met Maurice Richard and the Montreal Canadiens in the Cup final. The Habs whitewashed Toronto 6–0 in the first game, prompting Montreal's goaltending captain to wonder aloud, "How did these guys even make the playoffs?" Conn Smythe stormed into the Leaf dressing room flashing the headline and instructing his troops to give Bill Durnan an answer he would never forget. The Leafs returned to shut out the Canadiens in game 2 and finished them off in six games.

Still, Conn Smythe was not satisfied. He knew that he needed a dominant centreman to complement the play of Syl Apps and Teeder Kennedy. He saw that potential in Max Bentley and, in the biggest trade to that date in hockey history, dispatched five of his men to Chicago to bring the defending scoring champion to Toronto. He sent Ernie Dickens, Bob Goldham, Bud Poile, Gus Bodner, and Gaye Stewart to Detroit in exchange for Max Bentley and Reg Thomas.

Gordie Howe wrists one towards a screened Turk Broda during the first game of the 1948 finals. Leaf defenceman Garth Boesch guards Howe, who switches hands to fire this shot left-handed, a ploy he often used to confuse opposing goalies.

Imperial Oil Turofsky Collection, HHF

Howie Meeker is surrounded by Bruins as he attempts to one-time a pass into the yawning cage, March 22, 1948. Meeker was named the NHL's Rookie of the Year in the 1946–47 season after he set an NHL record by blasting home five goals on January 8, 1947, in a 10–4 pounding of the Blackhawks. Meeker coached the Leafs in 1956–57 and for one brief moment was general manager.
Imperial Oil Turofsky Collection, HHF

With Bentley on board and three solid lines supplying fire power, the Leafs cruised to the top of the league standings and sailed through the Stanley Cup playoffs. They crushed the Red Wings with surprising ease, taking a lead into the third period of every game and winning in four straight.

The Leafs lost one of their great leaders when Syl Apps decided to hang up the blades at the age of 33. Ted Kennedy replaced him as captain and the Leafs continued to fine tune their lineup by adding veteran Cal Gardner and youngsters Danny Lewicki and Tod Sloan. They looked great on paper,

Left to right: Les Costello, Vic Lynn, Hap Day, Ted Kennedy. "This picture was taken after we had eliminated Boston in the semi-finals in 1948. Les Costello was a very fine player with St. Mike's as a junior and played well with us on a couple of championship teams. He went into the priesthood and was one of the originators of the Flying Fathers, a hockey team made up of Roman Catholic priests who raised a lot of money for charity." — Ted Kennedy
Source unknown

Toronto Maple Leafs, 1948–49.
HHF Archival Collection

Syl Apps buries one behind New York Rangers' Chuck Rayner in 1947 action at the Gardens.
Imperial Oil Turofsky Collection, HHF

"When I joined the Maple Leaf hockey team Syl was captain of the club, and, next to Smythe and Hap Day, Syl perhaps deserved the credit, in my time, for establishing the standards for play and deportment within the Maple Leaf hockey team. He set the example for all us young fellows to follow, not only in his on-ice ability as a player and a leader, but off the ice in the way he conducted himself." — Ted Kennedy
Source unknown

Steady defenders Bill Barilko and Garth Boesch lost their sticks in this 1949 action. Turk Broda peers through the maze of arms and legs.
Imperial Oil Turofsky Collection, HHF

but on the ice it was a different story. They barely managed a spot in the playoffs of 1949. Then, unexpectedly, they steamed past the Boston Bruins in five matches, and knocked off the Red Wings in four straight games, becoming the first team in NHL history to win three consecutive Stanley Cups.

Dominant as the Leafs were in the 1940s, one can only wonder what they might have done had Smythe kept all the aces he had discarded along the way. He and Squib Walker had scouted such future stars as Elmer Lach, Bobby Bauer, Milt Schmidt, Woody Dumart, and Doug Bentley, but let them slip through their fingers on account of their diminutive size.

The Leafs entered the new decade confident they could continue their domination of the ice wars. With youthful understudies George Armstrong and Tim Horton appearing on the scene, and Al Rollins sharing the net with Turk Broda, they rose to third place and met the Red Wings in the semi-finals to pursue their fourth consecutive Stanley Cup win.

Bill Barilko lays the body on an unsuspecting attacker with an open-ice hit. Barilko claimed to be the toughest body-basher on the Leafs, a boast he proved in action.
Imperial Oil Turofsky Collection, HHF

Ted Kennedy, Conn Smythe, and Turk Broda share the joy of their 1951 Stanley Cup win with World War II veterans.
Imperial Oil Turofsky Collection, HHF

Captain Syl Apps is surrounded by a half-dozen Bruins during this 1948 playoff action. Apps retired after the 1948 season, despite the fact he was still young and had just enjoyed the finest season of his career. Smythe convinced Apps to return for the 1949 campaign, but when he learned that Hap Day had already appointed Ted Kennedy captain and wouldn't change his mind, Apps decided not to report, although Kennedy would willingly have stepped aside had Coach Day asked him to.
Imperial Oil Turofsky Collection, HHF

Coaches Joe Primeau and Hap Day and Captain Ted Kennedy present George Armstrong with Number 10, the sweater he made famous. Teammates Harry Watson, Jim Thomson, Sid Smith, and Howie Meeker look on. Armstrong first came onto the scene for a two-game trial in 1949 and in 1951 made the big club to stay; 1187 appearances later he was — and remains — the Leafs' all-time leader in games played.

Imperial Oil Turofsky Collection, HHF

Right from the start the series was fraught with drama. The Leafs were on their way to an eventual 5–0 win in the opening stanza when an incident occurred that would set the course for the entire series. Gordie Howe, while attempting to check Captain Ted Kennedy, crashed into the boards, suffering a severe head injury that required immediate surgery. Howe was on the verge of death for several hours while his teammates anxiously awaited word of their hero's condition. Everyone had a different opinion as to what exactly occurred, but the result was indisputable: Howe was out for the season and Kennedy was a marked man in Motown. In game 2 Kennedy was attacked by Fogolin, Lindsay, Abel, and the Detroit fans. So furious was their anger that NHL president Clarence Campbell stepped in with the threat of fines and suspensions were the fierce play to continue. The balance of the series featured hockey at its very best. Two of the games went into overtime, including the decisive seventh tilt. With the ailing Howe inspiring the Wings, they shut out the Leafs 1–0 with Leo Reise's overtime goal at 8:39 in the first overtime period. The Leafs' dream of a four-year dynasty had fallen one goal short.

George Armstrong

Right winger George Armstrong played more seasons and more games than any other Toronto Maple Leaf. "The Chief" first joined the team in 1949 and for the next 21 years wore the Maple Leaf.

At 6-foot-1, Armstrong's role was as a ferocious fore-checker. A steady team player, he kept the puck on Leaf sticks regularly, making perfect passes to his linemates, while giving opposing defencemen good reason to pause before checking him.

"Army" was captain of the Leafs from 1957 until 1969, when he passed the torch to Davey Keon, finally retiring in 1971. In his career he played a remarkable 1187 games and scored 296 goals and 417 assists while averaging less than 35 minutes per year in the penalty box. Under the guidance of this quiet leader, the Leafs won the Stanley Cup in 1962, 1963, 1964, and 1967, and though these years did not produce a superstar, Armstrong deserves the lion's share of the credit for keeping the aging team winning against all odds.

In 1975, George Armstrong joined the immortals in the Hockey Hall of Fame.

The 1949–50 Toronto–Detroit series was one of the fiercest Cup semi-finals ever played. Here a Leaf player lays on the body as the puck squirts loose.

HHF Archival Collection

"It was my birthday and they had a little celebration in Maple Leaf Gardens in our dressing room. I was 26 years old and I had 26 points. The people helping me eat the cake are Danny Lewicki (right) and Tod Sloan and Fern Flaman (left)." — Ted Kennedy

Source unknown

Ron Stewart does a hop, skip, and jump to escape the clutches of Bruins' defenceman Bill Quakenbush (Number 11) and Boston captain Milt Schmidt. Stewart was a relentless fore-checker and a compulsive workhorse whose hockey career stretched over 21 years in five different NHL locations. He skated with the Leafs from 1952 to 1965.

Imperial Oil Turofsky Collection, HHF

"This is Barilko's famous goal that won the 1951 Stanley Cup for us in the fifth game against the Montreal Canadiens. Each game in that series was settled in overtime. Barilko was a defenceman, and Joe Primeau was coaching us at the time. Bill was kind of a free spirit — he would gamble and take chances where other defencemen might not — and Joe was having a great deal of trouble keeping him back in his position. Bill saw the loose puck near the Canadiens' net and left his point position on the blueline, dashed in, and threw it up in the top part of the net to win the Cup for us. He skated back to the bench where Primeau was smiling and so happy. Barilko just looked at him and said, 'Joe, you didn't want a hook that time to keep me back there, did you?' It was a great moment, but the tragedy of it all is that Bill lost his life in a plane accident the following summer." — Ted Kennedy

Imperial Oil Turofsky Collection, HHF

The 1950–51 assembly racked up Maple Leaf records that still stand. The Leafs won 41 games and accumulated 95 points in the 70-game schedule. Gentleman Joe Primeau, whose trophy collection already included an Allan Cup and a Memorial Cup, now turned his attention to winning the biggest prize of them all. When Hap Day moved into the assistant manager's office, Primeau stepped in behind the bench. Among the veterans to leave the flock were Bill Ezinicki, who became a professional golfer; Vic Lynn, who was traded to Boston; and Garth Boesch, who went back to the family farm in Saskatchewan "to make some real money."

The Leafs finished the season in second place behind the Detroit Red Wings, who played their best hockey that year. Meeting the Boston Bruins in the semi-finals was a warm-up for what was to follow. They took the Bruins in five and went on to Montreal to meet Maurice Richard, Butch Bouchard, Doug Harvey, and the mighty Habs. Montreal had surprised all the experts by defeating a powerhouse Detroit squad which had managed 101 points in the 70-game season. Included in the Montreal victories were two wins in Detroit, both of which required more than three periods of overtime. The Habs were tired, but they had only seen the start of their after-hours duties.

Never before had a sporting event so drained the emotions of the country. Every minute of every game required the complete attention of every fan, who dared not blink or sneeze for fear of missing that all-important pass, the blistering shot from the point, or the closely watched offside. Three periods of hockey were not enough to contain these matches, and every one went into overtime. Sid Smith closed the curtains on game 1 at 5:51 of

"C'mon Teeder!" The deafening cry filled the Gardens every time Ted Kennedy would split the defence and leave a couple of opponents grasping at air. Here, Teeder dispatches Ed Sandford and Johnny Peirson on his way to the Boston net.

Imperial Oil Turofsky Collection, HHF

Conn Smythe had certain rules for his troops, one of which concerned players' getting married during the season. When Johnny "Goose" McCormack tied the knot in January 1951, the Major gave him an instant honeymoon in Pittsburgh, home of the Leafs' farm team. McCormack's days with the Leafs' organization were over when he was sold to the Canadiens on September 23, 1952.

York University Archives: Toronto Telegram Collection

overtime; Maurice Richard, the quintessential clutch player, sent the Leafs home at 2:55 of game 2's overtime; Ted Kennedy returned the favour at 4:47 of overtime in game 3; and Harry Watson turned out the lights in game 4 at 5:15 of overtime. Game five looked like it was pregnant with game six, as Montreal led 2–1 with fifty seconds left on the clock. Hap Day yanked Al Rollins from the cage, sending an extra attacker into the fray. Tod Sloan tied it up, sending the game into a fourth period. The final play of that fateful match is burned into the memory of all Leaf fans, young and old. Bill Barilko, hair flying, stretched to the limit, Richard and Bouchard frozen in time, the Leaf fans not yet able to react, the puck bending the twine above the falling Gerry McNeil. Sudden-death hockey is what overtime is all about — Barilko's shot marked the end of the game, the series, and the Leaf dynasty.

Bill Barilko scores in overtime to seize the Stanley Cup in 1951. This rare angle of that famous goal was discovered deep in the recesses of the Hockey Hall of Fame.
Source unknown

Cal Gardner (Number 17) wove his magic for the Leafs for only four seasons, but he was a big part of two Stanley Cup championships. He had the best seat in the house when Barilko potted the big winner in 1951.

Imperial Oil Turofsky Collection, HHF

Bill Barilko

He isn't listed on the honour roll at the Hockey Hall of Fame, and a search for his name through the Toronto Maple Leaf record book draws a blank as well. But Bill Barilko is very much a part of the history and mystique of the Toronto Maple Leafs. With his golden locks and California tan, "Bashing" Bill Barilko burst onto the scene mid-way through the 1946–47 season, looking like he came straight from Hollywood — which in a sense he did.

The Leafs first spotted Barilko in the hockey goldmine of Timmins, Ontario, and sent him to the Hollywood Wolves, their senior farm team in California. After hip-checking his way into the sports pages of Hollywood, Barilko was called north for a Stanley Cup screen test. His success in the spotlight was immediate, and the impact was felt by any opposing sweater who dared to cross the blueline in Barilko's general direction. After only 27 games with the Leafs Barilko was sporting a Stanley Cup ring.

Barilko became a fixture on the Leafs' blueline, battling and bashing his way into the hearts of the Toronto fans. The Leafs, with Barilko a vital spark, won three straight Stanley Cup championships from 1947 to 1949. After missing the finals in 1950 they returned to challenge Montreal in the 1951 playoffs. In the fifth game of that series, Barilko defied his coach and left his post on the blueline to fire home the Cup-winning marker in sudden-death overtime, still the most famous goal ever scored at the Carlton Street Cathedral.

It was to be Barilko's last game. He died that summer in a plane crash, and the fortunes of the team seemed to perish with him. His jersey, Number 5, has never been worn since. He is the only Leaf so honoured.

Sid Smith fires a low hard one at Bruins goalie Sugar Jim Henry, who just gets a toe on the puck. Smith had a 12-year career in Toronto and captained the team in the 1955–56 season.

Imperial Oil Turofsky Collection, HHF

The close of the 1950–51 season saw the end of an era in Toronto. It would be 11 long years before Toronto fans would gather again at city hall to celebrate Stanley Cup champions. Since the formation of the Toronto Maple Leafs Hockey Club in 1927, the team had made the finals twelve times and missed the playoffs on only four occasions. Even in those four years, the team felt little desperation: they were building years, when players, fans, and management knew that it would not be long before the club would rise again to its accustomed heights. But following the stellar goal by Bill Barilko, that was all about to change.

When Bill Barilko died in a plane crash in the summer of 1951, it seems that the spirit of the team died with him. On his return voyage from a northern Ontario fishing trip, his private plane was lost in the wilderness, and Barilko's body was lost with it. Not until his body was discovered in 1962 did the Leafs once again find the spirit that made them winners.

The youthful combination of Tim Horton and George Armstrong keeps Detroit rookie Norm Ullman under wraps. Armstrong and Horton both made brief appearances with the Leafs in 1949, and both saw action well into the seventies. They are the leading Leafs in games played at 1187 (Armstrong) and 1185.

Imperial Oil Turofsky Collection, HHF

Of course, it was not just the loss of Barilko that spelled doom for the franchise: many point to the Bentley trade, in which Conn Smythe sacrificed five talented men to achieve immediate success. Others look to the goaltending to find the cause of the dynasty's demise. They point to the Al Rollins trade, in which Smythe gave up five up-and-comers from the farm system to get Rollins, the best goalie in the AHL. He then traded four more regulars to replace Rollins with Harry Lumley. All this talent was sacrificed in a vain attempt to fill the skates of the greatest money goaltender of all time, Turk Broda.

Barilko is long remembered as the hero of the 1951 finals, but not enough credit has gone to Turk Broda. Broda had lost his number-one seating in the Leaf nets to Al Rollins, but when Rollins went down with a knee injury in the semi-finals, the Turk returned. In eight post-season games, Broda allowed only nine goals and registered a microscopic goals-against average of 1.12 — with two shutouts.

Turk Broda poses for the media, 1950.
Imperial Oil Turofsky Collection HHF

Turk Broda

There is one Leaf goaltender who should be placed on a pedestal above all the others. Hall of Famer (1967) Walter "Turk" Broda has been called the greatest money goaltender ever to strap on the pads, and his career record overwhelmingly supports that opinion. Turk appeared in 102 post-season games, compiling a microscopic 1.98 goals-against average and backstopping his mates to five Stanley Cup victories.

Conn Smythe discovered Broda by chance. During a scouting trip to Windsor to see a minor leaguer named Earl Robertson, canny Conn spotted the young Broda and liked him immediately. In 1936 Smythe bought Broda from the Detroit Red Wings and threw him into the fire the following winter. Broda responded by leading the NHL in victories and boosting the Leafs' tumbling fortunes. They would never miss the spring schedule again with Broda in the net.

Broda put in seven seasons with the Leafs before enlisting for two years. He then returned to reclaim his net from Frank McCool and tend it as the Leafs' money-man for another seven seasons.

Broda had always been somewhat overweight, but in 1950 he was not the only player in less than ideal shape. A health-conscious Smythe issued an ultimatum to the team, and Broda became the focus of public attention. He was benched with two weeks to lose either his *avoir dupois* or his net. His fans cheered him on with all manner of dietary advice, and Broda, always the man to come through in the clutch, was triumphant on weigh-in day, regaining his full share of the crease with newcomer Al Rollins.

That spring when Al Rollins succumbed to a knee injury, Broda responded with a playoff performance that would be his swansong. In the Stanley Cup finals he posted two zeros in nine matches, allowing only nine pucks beyond his grasp as the Leafs won their fifth Cup with the Turk in goal. Broda's name is still synonymous with that early era when the Leafs were at the height of their glory.

Sid Smith combs Detroit defender Marcel Pronovost's hair with his stick as Teeder Kennedy fires home a rebound past Terry Sawchuk. Smith spent 12 years with the Leafs (1946–1958), winning the Lady Byng Trophy twice. After a slow start — he spent most of his first three seasons in Pittsburgh with the AHL's Hornets — he had six consecutive 20-goal seasons. He was appointed captain in 1955 when Ted Kennedy retired, but when Kennedy returned the following season, Smith graciously passed the captaincy back to Kennedy.

Imperial Oil Turofsky Collection, HHF

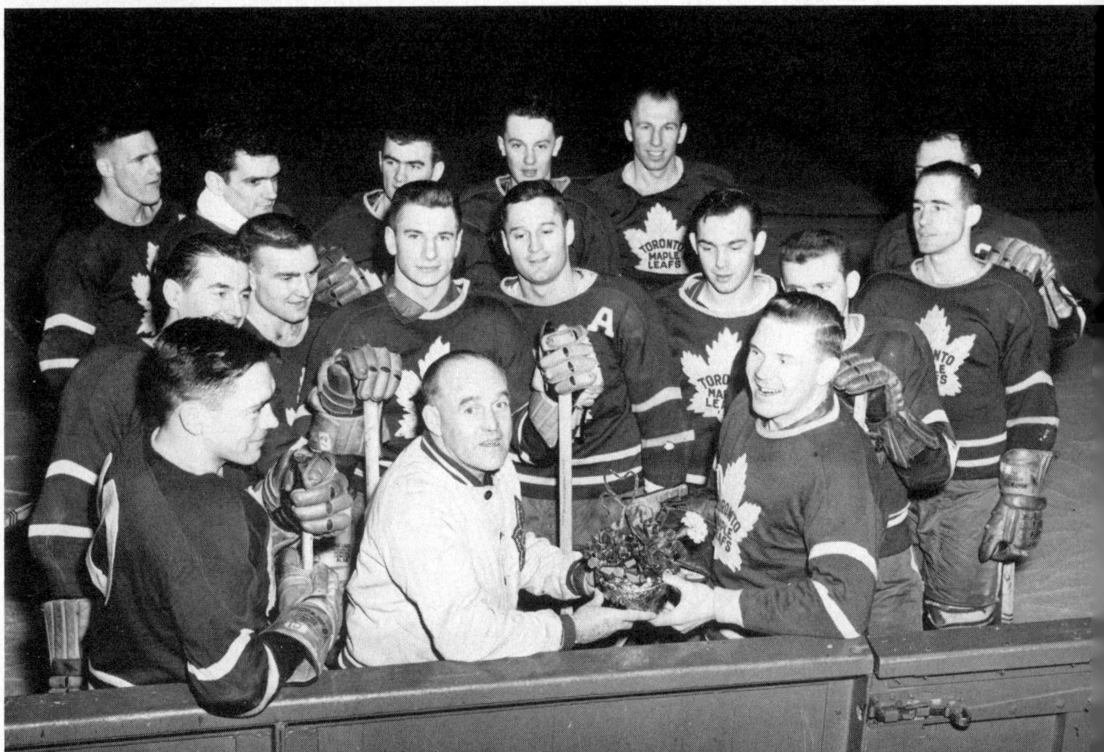

Harry Lumley presents Coach King Clancy with a St. Patrick's Day bouquet, 1955. After leading the Pittsburgh Hornets to the AHL crown, Clancy coached the Leafs from 1953 to 1956. Although he twice guided them into the playoffs, they were quickly eliminated on both occasions.

Imperial Oil Turofsky Collection, HHF

This scene was repeated all too often during the dismal days of the early 1950s. Gordie Howe has just buried one of his patented wrist shots past Harry Lumley, while Leaf defenders Jim Morrison (Number 21), Jimmy Thomson (Number 20), and Eric Nesterenko can only admire Howe's accuracy.
Imperial Oil Turofsky Collection, HHF

For the next six years, the team was mired in mediocrity. Some very good men wore the blue and white, but a winning unit never materialized. After being swept out of the playoffs in 1952, Smythe traded Gardner, Hannigan, Mortson, and Rollins to get Harry Lumley, but Lumley was not the answer. Max Bentley, discouraged and racked with pain, left the team and though he returned briefly, his defection wounded the team's spirit.

The Leafs missed the playoffs in 1953, but under King Clancy the following season rebounded to third place. Harry Lumley won the Vezina trophy, and established a Leaf record with 13 shutouts, but when the post-season rolled around, the same ghosts haunted the Leafs. In this case, It was the Detroit Red Wings, who again ousted them.

The farm system was still delivering new talent to the big club, and though on paper they were high-calibre hockey players, they lacked that intangible spark that had characterized the Leafs in their glory years. Smythe was still wheeling and dealing like a gambler on a roll, but the cards he drew were seldom as good as those he discarded. He gave up on Fernie Flaman, Leo Boivin, Harry Watson, Eric Nesterenko, and finally on the costly Harry Lumley. He received no players for these men, selling them outright. Smythe put the money into the farm system, but it would be a long-term investment that would not pay off until the next decade, when Smythe was no longer in a position to claim the credit.

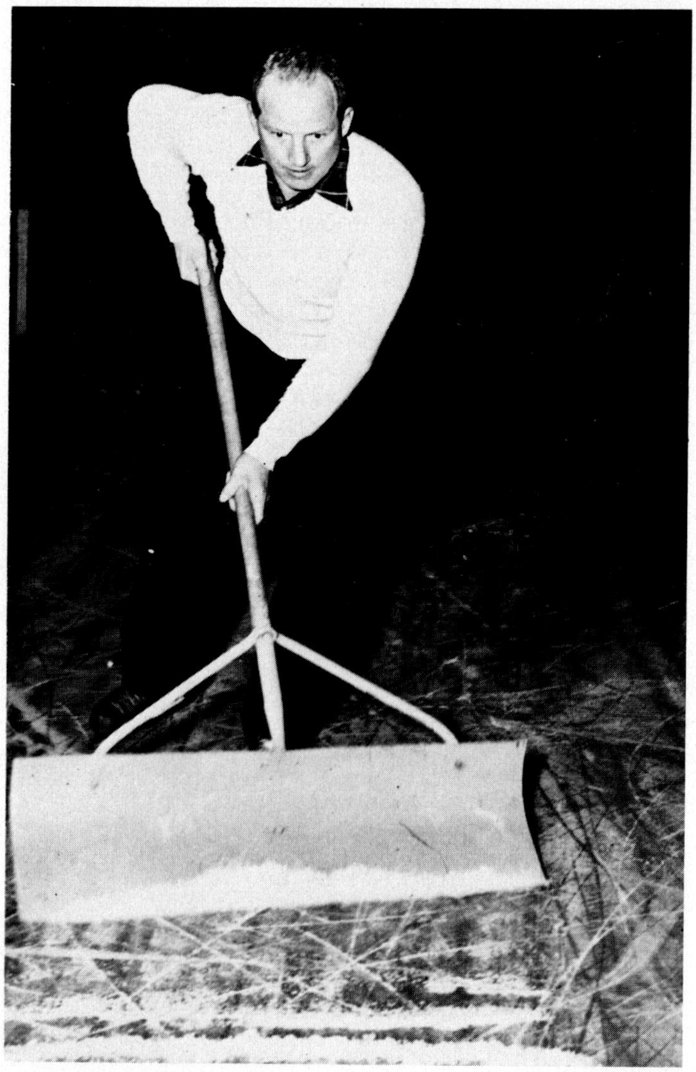

Hap Day shovelling. It has been said that Hap Day did every job with the Leafs but drive the Zamboni. That was before this picture turned up in the files of the Hockey Hall of Fame.
Imperial Oil Turofsky Collection, HHF

Ted Kennedy shows the drive that made him one of the all-time great Leafs as he forces the play in this 1957 match against Chicago. Ron Stewart stands off to the side of the crease, prepared for a rebound. Kennedy retired after winning the Hart Trophy in 1955, but returned in 1957 when the Leafs were slumping. He resumed the captaincy, but it wasn't enough to spirit the Leafs to the playoffs.

Imperial Oil Turofsky Collection, HHF

Harry Lumley with the Vezina Trophy.

HHF Archival Collection

March 20, 1957. Frank Mahovlich, wearing Number 26, plays his first NHL game, against the Montreal Canadiens. "This picture shows Doug Harvey, a defenceman who always had a hold of you or tried to grab your stick and made sure that all you got away with was your first shot. He was one of the reasons that Jacques Plante had such a great career." — Frank Mahovlich
Imperial Oil Turofsky Collection, HHF

The Leafs made the playoffs in 1955 but their exit was swift and humbling. Ted Kennedy retired after the 1956 campaign, leaving a gap that incoming captain Sid Smith was hard-pressed to fill. Howie Meeker was appointed coach for the 1956–57 season, but his tenure as pivot was no better than Clancy's had been. The Leafs missed the playoffs in both years, yet there was some light filtering through from the end of the tunnel. Bob Pulford, Bob Baun, Billy Harris, Carl Brewer, Bob Nevin, and a young kid from Timmins, Ontario, Frank Mahovlich, all emerged from the farm network to make their debuts with the Leafs in these years. They were the basis of the Leaf powerhouse of the sixties.

For all the difficulty the Leafs had replacing Turk Broda, they had equal trouble replacing Hap Day behind the bench. They tried Joe Primeau, King Clancy, Howie Meeker, and Billy Reay in turn, and with each the team declined further. The failures on the ice led to rapid and wholesale changes in the front office as well.

Since the exit of Frank Selke a decade earlier, Hap Day had gradually grown into the position of general manager, although he actually carried that title for only a brief period in 1957. He and Smythe had been friends and business partners for more than 39 years (Day had a hefty investment in Smythe's sand and gravel company), so it came as a shock to Day when Smythe indicated to the press after the Leafs missed the 1957 playoffs that he would be glad to see Day resign. Smythe appointed Howie Meeker as general manager — he wouldn't let Meeker coach the team again, saying, "All theory and no practice was Meeker's trouble; if he had a team made up of Rocket Richard and four more like him, he still couldn't win."

Frank Mahovlich takes a spill in front of Terry Sawchuk as Marcel Pronovost (Number 3) and Bill Gadsby (Number 4) look on.

HHF Archival Collection

Carl Brewer swept the Leafs' brass off their feet when he arrived during the 1957–58 season. Brewer was a rock-solid defender, who combined with Bobby Baun to form the original "Bash Brothers." After numerous clashes with Punch Imlach in the early sixties over money, politics, and players' rights, Brewer retired in 1965. In 1967 he was closely associated with Alan Eagleson in establishing the NHL Players Association. He returned in 1969 and was traded to Detroit, where he played one season. He then joined the St. Louis Blues for two seasons, retiring a second time in 1972. And in 1979–80 he returned to the Leafs once again at the age of 41 to play 20 games before retiring for the third and final time.

Imperial Oil Turofsky Collection, HHF

Smythe turned over control of the team to his son, Stafford, who had been honing his management skills with the Marlboros, which had long since been swallowed up by Maple Leaf Gardens Ltd. Stafford immediately fired Howie Meeker, saying he was far too young to be in such a position of power. Meeker's response is unrecorded. Stafford left the general manager's position nominally vacant, the empire being run by a group of seven men who came to be known as the "Silver Seven," suggesting that it took seven men to replace Conn Smythe. Stafford was chairman and obviously in charge. The other members of the group were Harold Ballard, John Bassett, George Mara, George Amell, George Gardiner, and Bill Hatch.

Stafford already knew that he wanted Punch Imlach, but Imlach was driving a hard bargain — he wanted to be general manager. Billy Reay filled in for 1957–58, but his coaching only served to convince Stafford that he should bend a little and bring on Imlach at all costs. Imlach, like Stafford, had done well in the minor leagues — he had gone from player to owner of the Quebec Aces — but was all but unknown in the NHL, although the Boston Bruins were courting him as well.

Stafford finally convinced Imlach to work for the Leafs, as assistant general manager, with the promise that he could earn his way into the vacant general manager's chair. The press had a field day. Just who was Punch Imlach? They laughed even more when Imlach's first player move was to sign an over-the-hill goalie from the roster of the Cleveland Barons of the American League. They laughed again when Imlach tried and failed to convince Guyle Fielder to leave the Western Hockey League and join the Leafs. But Imlach and Johnny Bower would have the last laugh.

Toronto started the 1958–59 season poorly, with Reay still behind the bench, winning only five of their first sixteen games. The Silver Seven had a conference on November 21 and invited Imlach to attend. They were discussing the Billy Reay situation, and asked Imlach's opinion. Punch said the Leafs were not playing for Reay, it was as simple as that. Following this meeting, Imlach was promoted to general manager. The press certainly enjoyed this, predicting that if the Leafs kept losing, Imlach would soon be named president.

Bob Pulford grimaces as his wrist shot dies in Jacques Plante's glove. Plante made his first appearance wearing a mask on November 2, 1959.

Imperial Oil Turofsky Collection, HHF

"I was down holidaying in Nassau when a fellow from Cleveland came up to me and started to talk about Johnny Bower when he played in Cleveland. They had nicknamed him the 'China Wall.' For many years with Toronto Johnny was a great leader and we always looked up to him." — Frank Mahovlich

Fitzsimmons Collection, HHF

Doug Harvey (Number 2) of the Habs holds his breath as Billy Harris rings one off the iron behind Jacques Plante in this 1958 action. Allan Stanley can be seen peering over Harvey's shoulder, beseeching the puck to deflect in the Leafs' favour. Harris joined the team in 1955 and was a key member of the championship Leaf teams of the sixties, playing on three Cup winners before moving on to Detroit in 1965.

Imperial Oil Turofsky Collection, HHF

When the Leafs continued to lose, Imlach fired Billy Reay and named himself coach with Bert Olmstead as his assistant. He immediately set out to restore the team's confidence with outrageous prediction for the club's success. He boldly claimed that the team would pass the New York Rangers and claim the last playoff spot, prompting Ranger coach Phil Watson to come back with, "Always he's predicting what the Leafs are going to do. The only crystal ball he's got is on his shoulders. What a beautiful head of skin!" Imlach might not have had a crystal ball, but that "beautiful head of skin" held the answers that Toronto had been in search of for nearly a decade.

On March 11, the Leafs were still seven points out of a playoff spot with only five games remaining. There were various combinations of Leaf wins and Ranger losses that would allow the Leafs into the post-season, but none of them was very likely. They met the Rangers on Toronto ice and shut them out 5–0; the following night at Madison Square Garden Bob Pulford scored in the final minutes to give the Leafs a 6–5 win and pull them within three points. They downed the Canadiens at the Forum 6–3 and the Hawks 5–1 back in Toronto. Meanwhile the Rangers, riding a five-game losing streak, finally won in Detroit. The next evening the Leafs would have to beat Detroit while the Rangers lost to Montreal in order to make the playoffs. Meanwhile, the NHL office, assuming the Leafs had no chance, had refused the Leafs permission to print playoff tickets! History tells us the Leafs came from behind to defeat Detroit 6–4 while the Rangers lost 4–2 to Montreal. Imlach, man of the hour at Maple Leaf Gardens, entered his first National Hockey League playoff round.

Ab McDonald (Number 15) climbs into the sin bin with Jean Beliveau and Frank Mahovlich. Maple Leaf Gardens was the first NHL arena to separate the combatants in the penalty box, although that innovation didn't occur until 1963. As this scene indicates, the guilty parties didn't always go to the cooler willingly, and once there, often continued the on-ice activity that led to their banishment.
Imperial Oil Turofsky Collection, HHF

Frank Mahovlich

One of the more enduring images for Leaf fans of the 1960s is that of Frank Mahovlich in full flight — picking up a pass at centre, gliding effortlessly over the blueline, and firing a cannonading shot past the opposing goaltender. "The Big M" connected on over 500 of those blasts in his career, which spanned 18 years in the NHL.

Mahovlich was born January 10, 1938, in Timmins, Ontario, where he demonstrated early an uncanny scoring ability. He moved to the OHA Junior A League in southern Ontario where he won the most valuable player award with the St. Michael's Majors, which brought him an invitation to skate with the Toronto Maple Leafs in a three-game trial in 1957. The Leaf brass, much impressed, signed him for the 1957–58 season, and he paid them back by winning the Calder Trophy that year. His star continued to rise when he potted 48 goals in 1961, and in 1962 he led the Leafs to their first Stanley Cup in 11 years.

Mahovlich reached true superstar status in October 1962, when Jim Norris, owner of the Chicago Blackhawks, offered $1 million for his services. The Leafs turned down the deal and Mahovlich was instrumental in Toronto's winning three more Stanley Cups in the sixties. In 1968, despite his numerous all-star appointments and his eight, 20-goal-plus seasons, Mahovlich was deemed expendable by the Leafs and was dealt to Detroit in one of the decade's blockbuster trades. Mahovlich seemed to be reborn in Detroit and turned in three productive campaigns with the Red Wings before finally joining the Montreal Canadiens, where he capped his career with some of his finest performances.

Mahovlich was often misunderstood; at times he seemed open and friendly, at others moody and taciturn. Both the media and the fans always felt that he could have done more, could have been so much better. However, his statistics speak volumes about the man and his abilities: 533 goals, 1103 career points spread over 18 NHL seasons, a nine-time all-star, the proud winner of six Stanley Cup rings, and election to the Hockey Hall of Fame in 1981.

Allan Stanley lays the lumber on Montreal Canadiens' rookie Ralph Backstrom in this 1959 action, while Captain George Armstrong attempts to clear away a rebound from the Leaf crease. Stanley joined the Leafs in 1958 after stops in New York, Chicago, and Boston. He was virtually booed off the Rangers, and his career seemed to be waning when Punch Imlach picked him up from Boston. He blossomed in Toronto and was a key member of four Maple Leaf Stanley Cup championship teams.
Imperial Oil Turofsky Collection, HHF

Punch continued his tack with the players, boasting that the Leafs would oust the Bruins in six games. No one seemed to mind that he was out by one: the Leafs took the Bruins in seven and entered the finals for the first time since the days of Barilko and Broda.

Imlach then forecast a Stanley Cup championship for the Leafs, foreseeing a seven-game victory. Alas, there were no more miracles that year; Montreal coach Toe Blake had the finest hockey talent on the face of the earth. The Leafs bowed to the powerhouse Canadiens in five games, but they had gained poise, confidence, and the feel of a winning club.

The Leafs rose to second place in 1959–60, and Imlach continued to tinker with the lineup to get just the winning combination. His game plan was to "put the kids in with a few old pappy guys who still like to win, and the combination is unbeatable." The Leafs made one of the best trade deals in their history, sending Marc Reaume to Detroit for aging defenceman Red Kelly. In a stroke of genius reminiscent of Conn Smythe's brilliant relocation of Hap Day from the front line to the blueline, Imlach moved Kelly to a forward line with Frank Mahovlich. The Leafs were off and running. They met the Canadiens again in the 1960 finals but were swept out in four straight. Despite the outcome, there was cause for great optimism in the Leaf camp. The Canadiens were aging, and the Leafs, with a strong contingent of young blood, seemed a likely successor to the Hab dynasty.

In the following year the Leafs made some important player changes. They added Davey Keon, Larry Hillman, Don Simmons, and a wild fan favourite from the Rangers, Eddie Shack. The hockey world watched closely as two of the league's best, Frank Mahovlich and Bernie Geoffrion, made a mad dash for the magical 50-goal mark. Mahovlich came up short, and despite Keon's Calder Trophy, Johnny Bower's Vezina, and Red Kelly's Lady Byng, the overconfident Leafs lost out to the Detroit Red Wings in the semi-final round of 1961 Stanley Cup play.

NHL president Clarence Campbell presents Dave Keon with his first Lady Byng Trophy. He won the Calder Trophy in 1961, the Lady Byng in 1962 and 1963, and the Conn Smythe Trophy in 1967. Keon, a Leaf from 1960 to 1975, spent only 117 minutes in the sin bin in his entire 22-year career. He made headlines during the 1974 campaign when he astounded his teammates on the final night of the season by taking on Greg Sheppard of the Bruins in a rare display of on-ice pugilism. The resulting five-minute penalty was the only major penalty Keon received in his professional hockey career.
Imperial Oil Turofsky Collection, HHF

Dave Keon

When Dave Keon was declared winner of the Calder Trophy in 1961, it was one of the most popular choices of all time. As Rookie of the Year he went on to set a shining example for the youth of the baby boom.

A steady scorer, Keon was a great team player who knew that he was more valuable on the ice than in the penalty box. In his 15 seasons with the Toronto Maple Leafs, he spent only 81 minutes in the sin bin, less than many of his contemporaries would rack up in a season or two. This two-time Lady Byng Trophy winner was the kind of hockey player that parents held up as an example to their children. In 1967 when he was surrounded by the national heroes who brought the Cup to Toronto, Keon was awarded the Conn Smythe Trophy as the most valuable man on the ice.

With the coming of the World Hockey Association, many NHL players were tempted to jump into the higher salary bracket. Keon, captain of the Leafs since 1969, was not keen to go, but problems with his salary negotiations led him to sign with the Minnesota Fighting Saints in 1975, where he continued to play like a champion. By 1979, the Hartford Whalers were a team of aging champions, and there Keon joined Bobby Hull and Gordie Howe to finish up his career.

This Hall of Famer (1986) will not soon be forgotten in Toronto, where he is much loved and respected for his exemplary years as the darling of the Maple Leafs.

Carl Brewer leaves his customary blueline spot to slip the puck between Glenn Hall's pads in this 1961 Leafs–Hawks battle. It was Brewer's only goal that year. Brewer's "palm-free" glove was an equipment alteration that allowed him to play the "clutch and grab" game to perfection, but when the NHL brass caught on, the "palm-free" glove was outlawed.

Imperial Oil Turofsky Collection, HHF

There was disappointment on more than one front, but Imlach's confidence in the team was so firm that he made virtually no revisions to the roster for the 1961–62 season. In fact the most important personnel changes did not involve players at all. On November 21, 1961, Conn Smythe sold the majority of his shares of Maple Leaf Gardens Ltd. to Harold Ballard, Stafford Smythe, and Johnny Bassett. Player moves were confined to the acquisition of Al Arbour and Eddie Litzenberger.

The Leafs finished in second place behind the Habs and cruised into the 1962 semi-finals against the New York Rangers, whom they had not met in post-season play since 1942. The Leafs easily won the first two matches. Then the Rangers came back to tie the series. At the end of regulation time in game 5 at Maple Leaf Gardens, the Leafs and Rangers were tied at 2's, when Red Kelly scored in overtime. Toronto finished off the Rangers in the sixth game, winning 7–1, and prepared to face the defending Cup champions, the Chicago Blackhawks.

The Hawks were strong from the goal line out with all-stars Bobby Hull, Stan Mikita, Pierre Pilote, and Glenn Hall in the lineup. Toronto boasted some fine talent, but the money was on the Hawks.

Johnny Bower

"I say he was the greatest athlete in the world and I don't care if anybody wants to argue it." Punch Imlach spoke these words about the ageless Johnny Bower in 1968. A decade earlier, few critics would have agreed with his assessment of the 34-year-old goalie who had spent the majority of his playing days in the minor leagues. However, 10 years later, when the venerable Bower was still turning back the firepower of the NHL's greatest snipers, no expert would have dared disagree.

After the 1957–58 season, a frustrating winter for the Leafs, Stafford Smythe drafted Johnny Bower from the roster of the Cleveland Barons. It's hard to say what sparked the most debate — Bower's talent or his age. No one seemed quite sure how old the veteran was, and Bower wasn't telling. He was known around minor-league dressing rooms as the "China Wall," giving some indication of his seniority in the ice wars. He had won every award available to a goaltender in the AHL and had tended the New York Rangers' net for a season (1953–54), but he had never really been given the chance to prove his worth in the NHL.

From the moment Bower stepped into the crease at the Gardens, he was outstanding. For years, the Gardens' enthusiasts had been waiting for a goalie who could match the legendary Turk Broda. Johnny Bower put an end to their wait. He led the NHL with the lowest goals-against average on three occasions and twice won the Vezina Trophy. Bower was a master with the goal stick, using it to poke-check an attacking rival or to bat away an airborne rebound. In the playoffs Bower was often unbeatable, playing those pressure-packed contests with the cool reserve that identifies a "money" performer.

Bower played 11 seasons with the Leafs, until the ripe age of 45, and was elected to the Hockey Hall of Fame in 1976.

This 1959 photo is a virtual Hall of Fame profile. Close examination reveals seven future Hockey Hall of Famers battling for the loose puck in this maze of 12 players, all but one of whom can be identified. The Leafs have pulled their goalie and are fighting for a tie, but only Red Kelly sees the puck. Moments later he sends the disc the length of the rink into the empty Leaf cage, giving the Red Wings a 4–2 victory. The players, from left to right, are Tim Horton, Bob Pulford, Frank Mahovlich, Gerry Ehman, Marcel Pronovost, Bert Olmstead, Gordie Howe, Warren Godfrey, Terry Sawchuk, Red Kelly, and Ron Stewart.

Imperial Oil Turofsky Collection, HHF

The odds makers took a beating after the first two games in Toronto, which the Leafs won 4–1 and 3–2. The Hawks came back to win a pair at home, with convincing 3–0 and 4–1 scores.

Johnny Bower was the undisputed master of the Toronto Maple Leafs net. His backup, Don Simmons, rarely got a chance to do more than practice. When Bower went down with a groin injury before game 5, Simmons went in and Leaf fans got the jitters. There was no need for doubts, however; the Leafs outplayed the Blackhawks 8–4 and 2–1, coming from behind in both games. After 11 years of struggle and disillusionment the Leafs had finally regained their place as champions of the world.

On June 6, 1962, bush pilot Gary Fields shouted: "There it is! There it is!" Bill Barilko's plane had been found, and later that summer his remains were laid to rest, buried with the memories of 11 dry years of Toronto Maple Leafs history.

Bob Pulford and Ranger goalie Gump Worsley search the skies for a flying puck as John Hanna (Number 6) comes to Worsley's aid. "Pully" spent 14 winters (1956–1970) patrolling left wing for the Leafs, and his trophy case includes four Stanley Cup rings. He went on to gain even greater renown as a coach and team builder with Los Angeles and Chicago.

Imperial Oil Turofsky Collection, HHF

The ageless Johnny Bower was an outstanding goalie, but even the "China Wall" sprung a leak or two on occasion. In this photo, Henri Richard eludes the famous Bower poke-check to fire one into the top shelf.
Imperial Oil Turofsky Collection, HHF

Once out of the woods, the Leafs took charge of the NHL, finishing the 1962–63 season in first place for the first time since 1947–48. They added Kent Douglas to the blueline crew and he immediately won the Calder Trophy. Davey Keon won his second consecutive Lady Byng, while Frank Mahovlich and Tim Horton made the all-star team. Bower allowed only 16 goals in the playoffs as the Leafs skated past the Canadiens and the Red Wings to the Stanley Cup for the second straight year.

Imlach was not one to tamper with success; Jim Pappin was the only addition to the roster in the fall of 1963. Mid-way through the season, however, the Leafs were stalled. When the lowly Bruins, at this time the doormats of the NHL, trounced them 11–0, and the Habs shut them out days later, Imlach moved. In a trade that rivalled the Max Bentley deal, the Leafs sent Duff, Nevin, Brown, Collins, and Seiling to the Rangers for Andy Bathgate and Don McKenney. Bathgate had been with the Rangers for 10 years, and had won the Hart Trophy in 1959. Heart is just what Imlach wanted from him, and he got it. Bathgate picked up 18 points in 15 games with the Leafs and pushed them into third place before the season had come to a close. They were ready for a showdown with their chief rivals, the Montreal Canadiens.

Red Kelly, wearing the captain's "C" in place of the injured George Armstrong, watches as Cesare Maniago bats the puck away. The Leafs acquired Kelly from Detroit in 1959 — arguably the most beneficial trade in Leaf history. They won four Cups with Kelly in the fold, and many historians point to the deal as the turning point for the team.
Imperial Oil Turofsky Collection, HHF

Conn Smythe turned over control of the Maple Leaf empire to his son Stafford in 1961.
Imperial Oil Turofsky Collection, HHF

Left to right (rear): Vic Stasiuk (11), Allan Stanley, Red Kelly, Marcel Pronovost (3), Norm Ullman(7), Bob Nevin; (front): Frank Mahovlich, Warren Godfrey (5), Terry Sawchuk "I think I scored on a backhand shot on Terry Sawchuk. Four of the five players on the Detroit Red Wings are back in position. It shows the defensive hockey that was played in those days. It was very difficult to score more than three or four goals in one game." — Frank Mahovlich

Imperial Oil Turofsky Collection, HHF

Frank Mahovlich. "When I came over from Detroit I was ten years older than Frank. They put us together; sometimes we played with Bob Nevin and sometimes with Gerry Ehman. Frank was a quiet sort of a chap, but on the ice he was a tremendous guy to play with. He had such a long reach and was a beautiful skater — and you always knew that Frank would find the holes if you could get the puck out to him." — Red Kelly

Imperial Oil Turofsky Collection, HHF

"Tim Horton was one of the strongest players I've ever known. I was fortunate to play on a team with him for 11 years. When I came to the Toronto Maple Leafs, Tim was one of the fellows I looked up to, and he was always giving advice that you could depend on." — Frank Mahovlich

Imperial Oil Turofsky Collection, HHF

Gerry McNamara guarding the gate for the Rochester Americans, one of the Leafs' main farm teams. McNamara played only seven games for the Leafs, but was to have a major role in the club's future, first as a scout and later as general manager during the eighties. The Rochester Americans and the Victoria Cougars were the main links in the Leaf system from 1957 until 1967 and 1968, when they were sold by Stafford Smythe, Harold Ballard, and John Bassett, who together controlled 60 per cent of the Leaf empire.

Fitzsimmons Collection, HHF

Bert Olmstead with Punch Imlach (left). "Bert was a very intense player. He was most effective along the boards and in the corners. He wasn't averse to giving a few instructions to his linemates when they needed it." — Red Kelly

Imperial Oil Turofsky Collection, HHF

Harold Ballard and Red Kelly, 1963. "In 1964, Harold sent champagne out to my house when we won the Stanley Cup. I wasn't there because they had taken me to the hospital, so I had missed all the celebrations. Harold brought a bottle of champagne, the Stanley Cup, and a photographer to my house. With my children, my wife, and the Stanley Cup, we had a picture taken. I don't know of anybody else who would have ever thought about doing that." — Red Kelly

Imperial Oil Turofsky Collection, HHF

Bobby Baun wheels around the Leafs' net with "Le Gros Bill," Jean Beliveau, in close pursuit. Baun was a chief factor in the Leafs' Stanley Cup wins during the 1960s, and his ferocious body-checking left many opponents bruised and bloody. Baun is best remembered for his overtime goal in the 1964 Cup finals, which he deposited behind Detroit goaltender Terry Sawchuk while skating on a fractured ankle.

Frank Prazak Collection, HHF

Dave Keon and Chicago tough guy Reg Fleming watch as the winning goal in the 1962 Stanley Cup playoffs finds the back of the Chicago net, ending 11 years of frustration for Leaf fans. The goal was scored by Dickie Duff, and although Keon didn't have a hand in it, he certainly helped by running interference with Hawks' goalie Glenn Hall.

Imperial Oil Turofsky Collection, HHF

Against the Canadiens in the semi-finals the Leafs fell behind 3 games to 2 but were able to battle back and win games 6 and 7 riding on the shoulders of great goaltending. Johnny Bower was sensational, allowing only one goal in the remaining two games and almost single-handedly pushing the Leafs into the finals.

The makeup of the Red Wings' lineup was similar to the Leafs'. Howe, Delvecchio, Pronovost, and Sawchuk had all tasted Stanley Cup champagne 10 years earlier, and with impressive youngsters like MacGregor, Crozier, and Henderson, the Wings were eager to taste the wine again. The Leafs were on their knees at the start of the sixth game, having lost three to Detroit. The champagne was on ice, and the Cup was waiting in the Detroit dressing room, when late in the third, with the score tied 3–3, Leaf defenceman Bobby Baun stopped a shot with his ankle and hobbled off to the dressing room. When the overtime call came, Baun was there, ready, willing, but barely able. After 2:43 of overtime, Baun drifted a shot toward the Detroit net, which somehow found its way past Sawchuk and into the cage. The Leafs had once more come back from the brink of elimination, and in game 7, Johnny Bower shut the door on the Wings' hopes. Andy Bathgate fired the winning tally, and Bobby Baun, playing on broken bones, provided the

Don Simmons puts his best foot forward to rob Chicago defenceman Pierre Pilote during the 1962 Stanley Cup finals. After Johnny Bower was injured prior to game 5, Simmons filled in and performed admirably as the Leafs won the remaining two matches to take the Cup. Pilote eventually ended up wearing the Maple Leaf in 1968, but stayed for only 69 games.

Imperial Oil Turofsky Collection, HHF

Bert Olmstead spies a loose puck on Johnny Bower's doorstep and makes a beeline to clear it out of the zone. Olmstead spent four seasons playing with the Leafs (1958–1962), retiring after Toronto won the Stanley Cup in 1962. He earned five Cup rings in his 14-year career in Montreal and Toronto.

Imperial Oil Turofsky Collection, HHF

inspiration for Keon, Kelly, and Armstrong's insurance markers. For the second time in their history the Toronto Maple Leafs had won the Stanley Cup three years straight.

Perhaps it was complacency, or perhaps it was Imlach's hesitancy to tamper with a smooth-running machine — in any case the Leafs remained virtually unchanged for the 1964–65 season. They did add Terry Sawchuk, although at the age of 35, his best years were behind him. Ron Ellis joined the squad, but the team was growing old, and it showed in the standings. Finishing fourth, the Leafs met the Canadiens, but unlike years past, there was to be no miracle. After six close games, the Habs emerged victorious and moved on to take the Cup.

For the 1965–66 season Imlach finally made a few changes. He surprised the Carlton Street faithful by unloading Andy Bathgate and Billy Harris; he added Marcel Pronovost, Larry Jeffrey, and youngster Brit Selby, who scooped up the Calder Trophy the following spring. But none of these players could shake the Leafs out of the doldrums. They were out in the first round. Eddie Shack gave the fans sparkle and entertainment — he didn't score many goals, but he wound up the crowd and kept them coming back to the rink.

"Red Kelly came to us from the Detroit Red Wings as an all-star defenceman. Imlach thought that he would be great up on forward so he played up for a number of seasons on a line with myself and Bobby Nevin. Red had great ability in passing the puck at the perfect time — and that was one of the big reasons why I scored so many goals with the Maple Leafs." — Frank Mahovlich

Source unknown

Eddie Shack. "They used to say that the only player in the National Hockey League that could skate down the ice full speed with a barrel between his legs was Eddie Shack. This picture reminds me of that." — Red Kelly

Imperial Oil Turofsky Collection, HHF

Opposing captains George Armstrong and Bob Nevin battle it out in front of the Leafs' cage while Tim Horton and Johnny Bower stand by in a 1964 game at Madison Square Garden. Nevin went to the Rangers along with Rod Seiling, Bill Collins, Dick Duff, and Arnie Brown in a blockbuster Imlach trade — all for 1959 Hart Trophy winner Andy Bathgate and centre Don McKenney. All five ex-Leafs continued to play high-calibre hockey for many more years, but Bathgate and McKenney only lasted two seasons in Toronto.

Frank Prazak Collection, HHF

Johnny Bower and Gordie Howe just after the Leafs defeated the Red Wings in game 7 of the 1964 Stanley Cup playoffs. The Leafs rebounded from the brink of playoff elimination to win the last two games and capture their third straight Stanley Cup. Holding the microphone is Frank Selke Jr., who, like his father, also tried his hand at managing, leaving the Canadiens organization to be the front office boss of the expansion California Seals.

Imperial Oil Turofsky Collection, HHF

Johnny Bower puts a stop to Norm Ullman's best-laid plans during this 1964 Wings–Leafs tilt at the Detroit Olympia. Bower teamed with ex-Detroit goalie Terry Sawchuk to win the Vezina Trophy in the 1964–65 season.
Frank Prazak Collection, HHF

The mood wasn't any more optimistic for the Over the Hill Gang in 1966–67. Brian Conacher was added, but it would be up to the veterans to make or break the season. The Leafs were in little danger of missing the playoffs: with the Boston and New York squads going through renovations, the team needed little more than a heartbeat to ensure post-season play. And heart was something the Leafs had plenty of. The men of the blue and white were the darlings of the city, and most of the country. They may have been aging heroes, but they were heroes nonetheless. They suffered through a 10-game losing streak and all bets were on a hasty departure from the playoffs. Imlach, staring failure in the face for the third straight year, checked into the hospital suffering from stress, leaving the team in the hands of King Clancy.

Eddie Shack, "The Entertainer," holds court behind the Leafs' net as John Ferguson of the Habs strolls behind him. Gary "Suitcase" Smith tends the cage for the Leafs. Smith, who played with the Leafs from 1965 to 1967, came by his nickname honestly: he wore eight different NHL jerseys in his career. Shack came to Toronto from the Rangers during the 1960–61 campaign. Known as the "clown prince of hockey," Shack was also a fine sharpshooter, scoring at least 20 goals for five different NHL squads in his 17-year NHL career.
Frank Prazak Collection, HHF

Toronto Maple Leafs, 1962–63. "We were very much like a family in those days, and I think it was the reason we won so many championships." — Frank Mahovlich

Imperial Oil Turofsky Collection, HHF

"As a kid, the first time in the Toronto Maple Leafs dressing room was a little awe-inspiring. Later, when I would look up and see the records of the Maple Leaf teams hanging on the wall, and what they had accomplished over the years, I felt it was something that gave you pride in your play." — Red Kelly

Imperial Oil Turofsky Collection, HHF

Leaf veterans Tim Horton (right) and Bob Pulford (left) put young hopeful Larry Keenan through his paces with a stickhandling drill which proves that everything is larger than life in the big leagues. The young Rochester American farmhand lasted only two games with the Leafs.

Imperial Oil Turofsky Collection, HHF

Dick Duff gets set to slip a backhander past Jacques Plante while being closely pursued by Tom Johnson (Number 10) and Don Marshall (Number 22). Duff made his first appearance with the Leafs late in the 1954–55 season and stayed for three Stanley Cup championships until he was dealt to the Rangers in 1964. He later joined the Canadiens where he played on another four Stanley Cup winners, becoming one of only three players to earn several Cup rings with different teams.

Imperial Oil Turofsky Collection, HHF

Bobby Baun

Harold Ballard once asked of no one in particular, "Ah, who remembers Bobby Baun anyway?" Baun was born in the prairie outpost of Lanigan, Saskatchewan, but his heart belonged to the Maple Leafs. He came east and toured with the Toronto Marlboros and the Rochester Americans before stepping onto the blueline for the Leafs in 1956. He stayed there for the next 11 years. In the 1967 expansion draft the Leafs lost Baun to Oakland, but he returned to Toronto to finish his career as a Leaf, retiring in 1973. He was known around NHL rinks as "Boomer," and he left more than a few opponents lying in a daze, wondering what had hit them.

The late fifties were growing years for both Baun and the Leafs, and when Baun was teamed with another youngster, Carl Brewer, the Leafs' fortunes took a considerable upswing. With Brewer and Baun, the original "Bash Brothers," on one line, and the venerable Allan Stanley and Tim Horton on the other, the Leafs presented a formidable defence that feasted on opposing forwards, who often ended up counting their bruises instead of their scoring points.

Baun served on four Stanley Cup winners, but it was during the 1964 showdown with Detroit that Boomer made his contribution to Leaf folklore. During the pivotal sixth tilt, with the Leafs down a game and hanging on by only a slim thread to Stanley Cup hope, Baun stopped a slapshot with his ankle. He barely made it to the dressing room, but refused the doctor's orders to quit for the night. He insisted that the doctor "freeze" his ankle — then he courageously limped back into the fray.

The game went into sudden-death overtime. With the freezing wearing off and the pain coming on, Baun took matters into his own hands. At the 2:43 mark, he lobbed a shot that skipped, slipped, and slid past a bewildered Terry Sawchuk, tying the series and giving the Leafs another life. Baun pulled on the blades for game 7 as well and, after a 4–0 Leaf victory, celebrated his third Stanley Cup win. Only later did it become known that Baun's ankle was broken. To answer Ballard's question with a question: who could ever forget that April night in 1964 when Bob Baun scored one of the most famous goals in Stanley Cup history?

Stanley Cup Parade, Toronto, 1964.
Imperial Oil Turofsky Collection, HHF

Andy Bathgate is swarmed by Montreal Canadiens Jean-Guy Talbot, Ted Harris, Charlie Hodge, and Claude Provost in December 1964. It took at least that many players to stop the crafty Bathgate who came on board during the 1963–64 season and provided the Leafs with the much-needed spark that fired them towards a third straight Stanley Cup.
Frank Prazak Collection, HHF

The Toronto Maple Leafs, 1963–64. First row: Punch Imlach, Allan Stanley, Stafford Smythe, George Armstrong, Harold Ballard, Bob Pulford, King Clancy. Second row: Dave Keon, Ron Stewart, Johnny Bower, Don Simmons, Tim Horton, Bobby Baun. Third row: Carl Brewer, Frank Mahovlich, Andy Bathgate, Red Kelly, Billy Harris. Fourth row: Bob Haggert, Eddie Shack, Jim Pappin, Don McKenney, Larry Hillman, Tommy Nayler.

HHF Archival Collection

Imlach was a drill sergeant, but Clancy by this time was pretty laid back. He knew his men were seasoned and understood what had to be done, and he stepped back and let them do it. Under Clancy the veteran Leafs found their second wind, bringing home nine consecutive victories. When Imlach returned with his own second wind, he found a changed hockey club, one whose spirit reminded him of the team he had taken over 10 years previous, and he looked for one last miracle.

Mid-way through the 1966–67 schedule, the Leafs hit a record ten-game losing streak, and Punch Imlach had to be hospitalized to recover from trauma and strain. King Clancy stepped into the breach behind the Leafs' bench, and the team turned around and won the next nine games, climbing into the playoff picture and staying there. When Punch returned, the Leafs were much more relaxed and had a new winning attitude that carried them to playoff victory.

Imperial Oil Turofsky Collection, HHF

Jim Pappin led the Leafs in scoring in the 1967 playoffs but fell foul of Punch Imlach the next season. He was then dealt to Chicago where he spent seven productive seasons, averaging over 30 goals a year. The Leafs received all-star defenceman Pierre Pilote in return, but Pilote's best years were behind him and he retired after only 69 games in a Leaf uniform.
Frank Prazak Collection, HHF

When the Leafs met the Chicago Blackhawks in the 1967 semi-finals, odds were on the Hawks to win, Chicago having led the league in goals scored and goals against. Toronto lost the first game to Chicago 5–2, and early in the second game, Terry Sawchuk stopped a Bobby Hull slapshot with his mask. The trainer rushed to his side and asked Sawchuk if he was injured. Sawchuk replied, "Well, I stopped it, didn't I? Now let's play some fuckin' hockey!" This stop marked the turning point of the series as Bower and Sawchuk shut down the Hawk attack, holding them to only seven goals in the remaining five games.

The Leafs designed a new uniform for the playoffs. The new logo was a stylized maple leaf based on the centrepiece of the new Canadian flag. With the new leaf emblazoned on their chests, the Leafs skated out for the Centennial year showdown with the Canadiens.

Terry Sawchuk, Bob Pulford, Pete Stemkowski, and Larry Hillman crowd Phil Esposito of the Blackhawks in the 1967 semi-finals. The Hawks led the NHL in almost every category, both offensive and defensive, and it was one of hockey's great upsets when the Leafs ousted Chicago in the 1967 post-season.
Frank Prazak Collection, HHF

In the mid-sixties when Harold Ballard was executive vice-president of Maple Leaf Gardens, he began to bring big-name entertainers to the Gardens. The Beatles, Frank Sinatra, Muhammad Ali, and Bob Hope, were among the stars who drew capacity crowds and pushed up Gardens stock till it split five for one in 1965.

Imperial Oil Turofsky Collection, HHF

Punch Imlach, 1967. "Punch Imlach turned me professional as a 19-year old. Ironically, it was also Punch Imlach who was back as GM of the Maple Leafs when I retired from hockey. He was with me in the beginning and with me at the end. What I remember most is his ability as a bench coach. I don't believe that there were too many other coaches in the NHL who handled a bench as well as Punch. He knew how to match lines and change lines extremely well, and that was one of his strengths."— Ron Ellis

Source unknown

Johnny Bower and Bobby Baun seem to strike a prayerful attitude as Larry Hillman tries to remove Detroit's Floyd Smith from the Toronto crease. On many nights Bower's prayers were answered as the Leafs dominated the NHL during the early years of the 1960s.

Imperial Oil Turofsky Collection, HHF

Pete Stemkowski (Number 12) goes for a spill in front of Montreal goalie Rogie Vachon, courtesy of Jacques Laperriere, who is also down. The 1967 finals featured great performances from "Stemmer" and his linemates. Jim Pappin (Number 18) led all scorers in the post-season, and Bob Pulford's (Number 20) overtime marker in game 3 gave the Leafs the series lead.

Frank Prazak Collection, HHF

Both the Toronto Maple Leafs and the Montreal Canadiens were national legends and Stanley Cup fever was at its highest pitch ever. They met for game 1 in the historic Montreal Forum, where the Leafs were blasted back to the dressing room in a 6–2 routing. Sawchuk had injured his ankle and was replaced by Bower in the third period. For game 2, Johnny Bower, by now 42 years old, faced a freshly scrubbed 21-year-old Rogie Vachon, whom Punch Imlach described as a "junior B" hack. The China Wall lived up to his moniker, shutting out the Montrealers 3–0.

When the Leafs returned to Toronto, they were already being hailed as living legends. In the pivotal third game Johnny Bower stopped 54 of the 56 shots blasted his way, and when Bob Pulford took a centring pass from Jim Pappin at 8:26 of the second overtime period, the Leafs took control of the series. Bower suffered a groin injury in the warm-up for game 4, and Terry Sawchuk was called upon to deliver the miracle. The Gardens faithful moaned as Sawchuk allowed six Montreal markers and the teams returned to the Forum, tied at 2's. Terry Sawchuk had not known the taste of Stanley Cup victory since 1955, and he knew he would never be this close again. The Leafs skated onto the Forum ice and, led by Brian Conacher, stunned the Habs with an easy 4–1 victory, sending the series back to Toronto for the final showdown.

Frank Mahovlich pursues a loose puck while Montreal's Ted Harris attempts to hamper his progress during the 1967 Stanley Cup finals. Although every Leaf fan suffered with Mahovlich when he was traded to Detroit in 1968, the move resurrected his career and enabled him to produce the kind of hockey everyone knew he was capable of. Mahovlich is one of only three players to win at least two Stanley Cups with two different teams. He picked up four Cup rings with the Leafs, and then after three seasons in Detroit he went to Montreal, where he was the Habs' offensive sparkplug for two more Cup wins in the early 1970s.

Frank Prazak Collection, HHF

Toronto Maple Leafs, 1966–67, winners of the Stanley Cup. "We had a very seasoned team, a lot of veterans who were able to reach down and use the tremendous experience they had gained from their other Stanley Cup wins to win a series we weren't supposed to win, to win a Stanley Cup when we weren't even considered to be contenders. It was strictly because of the character of the team." — Ron Ellis

Toronto Maple Leafs Hockey Club

"When we won the Stanley Cup in 1967 it was the last year of the old six-team format. Terry Sawchuk and Johnny Bower were two of the key reasons we won the Cup. Sawchuk challenged the shooters in all the games he played. My most vivid memory of Terry is when he challenged Bobby Hull and really frustrated Bobby during the semi-final series. He showed such tremendous courage." — Ron Ellis

Frank Prazak Collection, HHF

Ron Ellis tests Boston goalie Eddie Johnston from the doorstep while Dean Prentice (Number 17) and Ed Westfall (Number 18) look on. Ellis spent his entire NHL career (1963–1981) with the Leafs, and he scored 20 or more goals in 10 consecutive seasons. He retired briefly after the 1975 campaign, but returned two years later to play a key role in the revitalization of the team.

Frank Prazak Collection, HHF

Tim Horton

When the Toronto Maple Leafs won their four Stanley Cups during the 1960s, they did it with a strong wall of defence — anchored by Tim Horton. Horton graduated to the Leafs from the St. Michael's Juniors, and although he made his first appearance in the blue and white in 1949, the Leafs sent him to one of their farm teams, the Pittsburgh Hornets of the AHL, to perfect his craft. He helped the Hornets to the Calder Cup championship in 1952 and won an AHL all-star appointment. The following season, the Cochrane, Ontario, native joined the Leafs where he was a fixture behind the blueline for the next 18 seasons.

Although at 5-foot-10 and 180 pounds Horton was not a big man, he was often in the middle of the fray, wrapping up his enemies in the infamous "Horton Bear Hug." When he was teamed with Allan Stanley prior to the 1958–59 campaign, the Leafs found the defensive pairing that led them to the Stanley Cup four times.

The Toronto Maple Leaf record book still echoes Tim Horton's many achievements. His resilience allowed him to play six consecutive seasons (1961–62 to 1966–67) without missing a game, a Leaf record that still stands. He was an NHL all-star on six occasions, five of them during his remarkable "ironman" streak, and his 1185 games played for the organization places him only two behind all-time leader George Armstrong.

The Leafs eventually traded Horton to New York in March 1970. He played four more years of excellent hockey. After a year with the Rangers he put in a season with Pittsburgh. He then went to Buffalo where he was finishing his second season when he was killed in an auto accident at the age of 44.

Horton was much loved by Leaf fans and always received a tremendous ovation whenever he skated onto the Gardens ice, regardless of the uniform he was wearing. His achievements were honoured with election to the Hockey Hall of Fame in 1977.

One of the biggest trades in NHL history occurred when the Leafs unloaded Frank Mahovlich on March 3, 1968. The "Big M" was sent to Detroit with three others in return for Norm Ullman, Paul Henderson, and Floyd Smith. The Wings later traded Mahovlich to Montreal, where he helped the Habs win two Stanley Cups. Ullman was a key figure for the Leafs after the trade, leading the team in scoring for three of his first four years.

Frank Prazak Collection, HHF

Toe Blake started Gump Worsley in the Montreal net for the sixth game, but he could not stem the tide. After second period markers by Ronny Ellis and Jim Pappin, the Gardens fans stood poised for the kill. Dick Duff made a brilliant solo dash early in the third period, leaving Tim Horton and Allan Stanley gasping for air and firing past Sawchuk to pull the Habs within one goal of salvation. After Montreal forced a last minute face-off in the Leaf zone, Blake yanked Worsley and sent out an extra attacker. Imlach sent out Horton, Armstrong, Pulford, and Red Kelly, all old geezers by hockey standards. Then he did the unthinkable: he sent Allan Stanley, an aging defenceman, out to face off against "Le Gros Bill," Jean Beliveau. Stanley won the draw and passed to Pulford, who spotted George Armstrong in the clear. Armstrong stepped over centre ice and fired the puck into the centre of the yawning cage. For the eleventh time in their history, the Toronto Maple Leafs would have their names engraved on the Stanley Cup.

As the delirious fans poured out onto Carlton and Yonge, they echoed the delight felt by those earlier Toronto fans who hailed their victorious Toronto Blueshirts in 1914. Since that first taste of victory, Toronto had savoured this ultimate sporting victory 14 times.

The demise of the Toronto Maple Leafs after 1967 has been well documented and lamented elsewhere. It is not the aim of this book to repeat the story here, but neither can the causes of the fall from grace be ignored. While it is true that the team has not found the mark since 1967, it is important to keep this in perspective. Only two "original six" teams have won Cups since that time, and only six different teams have done so in total. the "expansion years" have also been "dynasty years," different teams taking turns at dominating NHL play. The Leafs' sudden fall and long interment may be accounted for by several factors, but there are a few that stand out as key.

The Bathgate trade which sent youth to the ailing Rangers was certainly not in the Leafs' long-term best interests. While Bathgate played only 70 games for the Leafs, the players they gave up played for a total of 61 more years! Dick Duff went

Jacques Plante peers anxiously through his famous mask as Leaf defenceman Jim Dorey takes care of crease invader Bill Hicke. Plante joined the Leafs in 1970, compiling an incredible goals-against average of 1.88, and tossing in four shutouts for good measure. He stayed with the Leafs until mid-way through the 1973 campaign. Jim Dorey played with the Leafs from 1968 to 1971 and was a hot-headed young man who, in his first game at Maple Leaf Gardens, set an NHL record for penalties in one game, racking up nine infractions of all types.
Graphic Artists

The Leafs returned to the playoffs in 1969, only to be humiliated by Boston. The Bruins won the first two games on home ice with scores of 10–0 and 7–0, then completed the sweep with 3–2 and 4–3 victories in Toronto. Here, Derek Sanderson and Eddie Shack attack Johnny Bower, Tim Horton, and Ron Ellis in game 4, on April 6, 1969. After more than a decade behind the bench, Punch Imlach was fired following this game.
Frank Prazak Collection, HHF

The Leafs received Paul Henderson in the Mahovlich trade of 1968, and he was a steady though unspectacular performer with the team for six and a half seasons. It was Henderson's "shot seen round the world" for Team Canada '72 that made his name a household word.
Frank Prazak Collection, HHF

on to play another nine years in the NHL, winning two Cups with Montreal; Rod Seiling played 16 years of big-league hockey; Bob Nevin shot and scored for 14 more years, and Arnie Brown stabilized bluelines for 11 further seasons. At the time, Bill Collins was the no-name player involved in the deal. When the NHL expanded in 1967 Collins got his chance and he skated in NHL rinks for 11 winters. None of these players are likely to find their way into the Hockey Hall of Fame, but they were role players, and Leaf teams have always needed their like.

The selling of the farm teams in Rochester and Victoria, British Columbia, by Stafford Smythe and Harold Ballard in 1967 and 1968 cannot be underestimated. The organization lost 45 NHL-calibre players, and it has often been said that the Rochester Americans of the mid-sixties were strong enough to play in the big league. By 1968 the Leafs were virtually without any minor-league talent. It had been the mark of Conn Smythe to find and nurture young players, but this was no longer a priority of the team's owners.

One crack in the foundation was beginning to show as early as 1965. When the Leafs had been unsuccessful in the 1950s the changes came fast and from the top down, yet Punch Imlach was left in control of the team despite the clearly impending doom.

Mid-way through the 1967–68 season, with the Leafs floundering and gasping for playoff air, Imlach orchestrated a trade that nearly caused riots in the streets of Toronto. He sent Frank Mahovlich to Detroit for Norm Ullman, Paul Henderson, and Floyd Smith. These three would serve the Leafs valiantly for many years, but they were only three men. The key to the Mahovlich trade was the youth that Imlach gave away. Along with Mahovlich went Peter Stemkowski, Carl Brewer, and Garry Unger, all men with many years yet to play.

The team showed improvement in 1968–69, finishing in fourth place to meet Boston in the quarter-final round of the newly expanded NHL playoff system. The Leafs lost the first two games by a combined score of 17–0, and when Boston skated off Gardens ice on April 6, 1969, after sweeping the Leafs unmercifully from the playoffs, it marked the end of an era in Toronto. Punch Imlach had held his cards too long and was fired immediately following the game. Management set out to rebuild the team in the manner that had been so successful in previous ages.

Dave Keon, 1973. "I considered it a privilege to play on the same team as Dave Keon. One thing I'll always remember about Davey as a captain and as a team member is that he led by what he did on the ice. That was his strong suit. His work ethic and his ability to get up for the big games put him heads above other players." — Ron Ellis
Source unknown

Ron Ellis played 16 seasons for the Leafs. His quiet yet effective leadership led Ace Bailey to request that Ellis be permitted to wear Number 6, Ace's old number, which had been retired since his injury in 1933.
Frank Prazak Collection, HHF

Darryl Sittler clashes with Habs' Claude Larose.
Frank Prazak Collection, HHF

Progress was slow and difficult. With the farm system dry, manager Jim Gregory and new coach Johnny McLellan had their work cut out, finding new talent in an already overextended National Hockey League player pool.

The Leafs missed the playoffs in the 1969–70 season, but took some consolation that the defending Cup champion Montreal team was also absent in the post-season. The Leafs still had Pulford, Keon, Armstrong, and Ellis, and had added Brian Glennie, Rick Ley, Jim Dorey, and Murray Oliver. It was a building year, and the Leafs used their first-draft selection to bring in Darryl Sittler, whom they hoped would turn the table on the current gloom.

Mike Pelyk was rushed unsteadily into the Leafs' picture in 1968. His coming of age during the Leafs' losing years was often a painful experience, but by 1973 he had developed into a front-line blueliner and had a career year in 1973–74. Then the Leafs lost him to the money-mongers of the World Hockey Association.
HHF Archival Collection

Errol Thompson, the pride of Summerside, Prince Edward Island, scores as goalie Cesare Maniago, Bruce Boudreau (Number 19), and Jack McIlhargey (Number 29) look on. Thompson scored 43 goals in 1975–76, leading the team in goals scored.
Source unknown

The Leafs jumped over the .500 mark in 1971 with Norm Ullman and Dave Keon both enjoying the finest years of their careers. An added boost was the purchase of Jacques Plante's contract from the St. Louis Blues. Plante was happy in Toronto, finishing the season with a league-leading goals-against average of 1.88, an incredible accomplishment for the 41-year-old veteran. Plante shared the net with a promising youngster, Bernie Parent, whom the Leafs had acquired in February from Philadelphia. Parent remained in the Leaf fold through the 1971-72 season, but it was evident that he was unhappy with the progress of his contract talks.

Harold Ballard was now majority owner of the Leafs, and a storm was brewing on the horizon. The World Hockey Association (WHA) was formed, signalling the start of an all-out money war with the NHL, a battle Ballard was not prepared to fight. In March of 1972, Bernie Parent became the first name player in the NHL to jump ship and join the pirates. Ballard was prepared to engage in hostilities, but not to pay the price of admission, while WHA dollars floated around the league like manna from heaven.

The WHA battle roared on for the remainder of the decade, with Ballard and the Leafs losing many good men, including Keon, Stoughton, Ley, Henderson, Ullman, Favell, and Pelyk. Many teams felt the effects of this eight-year pillage of talent, but Ballard's refusal to match dollars with the opposition robbed his team of the men who could have turned the tide in the Stanley Cup regatta.

Even in the midst of the WHA wars the Leaf rehabilitation continued. By 1973 the Leafs began to find players that would make a difference. They drafted Lanny McDonald and Ian Turnbull, and the next season added Dave "Tiger" Williams and Mike Palmateer. Though the team was having only limited success on the ice, it was clear that the nucleus was there. The 1973–74 campaign was one of the most successful in years. Red Kelly was named coach and led the team to a 35–27–16 mark, good for fourth place in the NHL Eastern Division. The previous year, chief scout Gerry McNamara had seen two young players with the Swedish National

Ian Turnbull, the man Harold Ballard "wouldn't trade for God," had the greatest night of his career as a member of the Leafs, setting an NHL record for a defenceman by scoring five goals against Detroit on February 2, 1977.

Miles S. Nadal Collection, HHF

A spark was added to the Leafs lineup in 1974 when Dave "Tiger" Williams roared into town. The Tiger was a rambunctious crowd-pleaser whose rowdy nature — he racked up 1670 penalty minutes in seven seasons with the Leafs — was complemented by solid scoring ability.

NHL Services

In one of their wisest investments, the Leafs signed a young defenceman out of Sweden in 1973. Borje Salming went on to anchor the Leafs' defence for 16 seasons, establishing himself as the finest European blueliner ever to skate in the NHL.
Miles S. Nadal Collection, HHF

team, and in a rare coup signed Inge Hammarstrom and Borje Salming.

The Leafs went into the 1974–75 campaign with a new optimism and a strong lineup. They engineered one of their greatest playoff upsets, eliminating the Los Angeles Kings, who had finished the season 27 points ahead of the Leafs, in the preliminary round. Though they would lose in straight games to the eventual Cup-winning Philadelphia Flyers, it was evident that the rebuilding was sound.

In the following year Darryl Sittler and Lanny McDonald emerged as NHL superstars. Though the team finished only three games over .500, the line of Sittler, Errol Thompson, and McDonald racked up 273 points, with Sittler becoming the first Leaf player to record 100 points in a season. The 1975–76 campaign also saw the most exciting performances in recent Leaf history. Darryl Sittler established a new high-water mark for NHL play that stands to this day. On February 7, 1976, Sittler scored six goals and added four assists for 10 points in an 11–4 victory over the Boston Bruins.

The Leafs continued to impress the fans in post-season performances, stretching the Philadelphia Flyers to a seven-game series, which ranks among the most breath-taking ever played in Maple Leaf Gardens. On April 22 Darryl Sittler tied an NHL record, scoring five goals in an 8–5 Toronto win. Though the Leafs lost the series, they gave the fans something to talk about over the summer months and great hope for the following season.

Darryl Sittler had one of the best nights of his career against the Boston Bruins on February 7, 1976.
HHF Archival Collection

Borje Salming

When Gerry McNamara returned from a scouting trip to Europe in 1973, he recommended to the Leafs a talented young defenceman from the Swedish National Team. Borje Salming's signing on May 3, 1973, was regarded as little more than a publicity manoeuvre for the floundering Leafs, and few critics expected much from the unknown Swede. To McNamara's everlasting credit, Salming became the finest European defenceman ever to play the North American game.

Salming's first NHL season was trying. He was subjected to both physical and psychological abuse, but he persevered. By 1974–75, he was an NHL all-star, an honour he was to receive for six consecutive seasons and a record for a Toronto Maple Leaf. He set numerous other team records, including career assists, season assists for a defenceman, all-star team nominations, and career goals by a defenceman. His 1099 games played with the Leafs ranks him third on the team's all-time games-played list.

The free-wheeling flair that characterized Salming's early years gave way to a more conservative, stay-at-home style of play in the 1980s. Though his offensive numbers suffered, he was often the Leafs' top plus/minus player, proof that the transition was both beneficial and successful. Salming put team performance ahead of personal glory, sticking with the Leafs despite the frustrations and losing seasons in the 1980s. However, at the end of the 1988–89 season he was successfully wooed by Detroit. Whenever "B.J." decides to hang up the blades, there will no doubt be a spot for him in the Hall of Fame.

In 1976 the line of Errol Thompson (left), Darryl Sittler (centre), and Lanny McDonald racked up a Leaf record of 273 points, with Sittler becoming the first Leaf to reach the 100-point plateau in a single season.
NHL Services, R. Shaver

Darryl Sittler, 1975. "Here was a player that should have played only for the Toronto Maple Leafs. He was not only a great hockey player but a tremendous team player. He was a leader who wouldn't tell you what to do — he would go out and show you how it should be done. Darryl could do it all — shoot, pass, skate — and if he had to he could really take care of himself. We played on the same line for four and a half years and shared a lot of great moments together. But more important to me is the fact that Darryl is my best friend." — Lanny McDonald
HHF Archival Collection

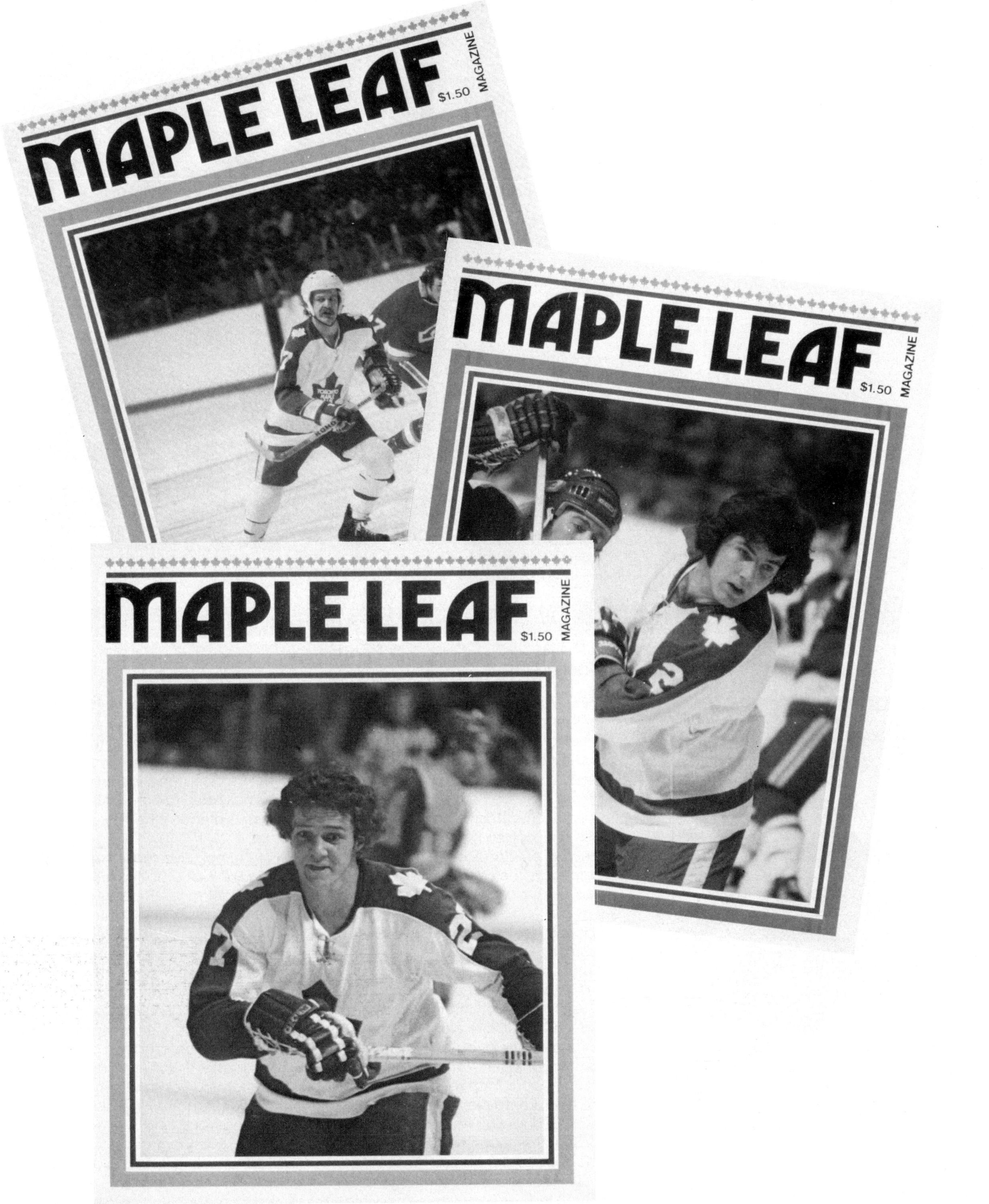

Leaf program collage, 1975. Top to bottom: Lanny McDonald, Ian Turnbull, Darryl Sittler. This trio of clever draft picks led the team throughout the seventies.

Maple Leaf Gardens, HHF Archival Collection

Mike Palmateer
Robert Shaver,
HHF Archival Collection

Darryl Sittler

The 1970s was a decade of contrasts for the Toronto Maple Leafs. It was a time both of triumph and of trauma from which one man, more than any other, emerges as one of Toronto's greatest on-ice heroes.

After an outstanding junior career with the London Knights, Darryl Sittler, a native of Kitchener, Ontario, was drafted by the Leafs in 1970. Toronto was in a rebuilding phase, and Sittler was allowed to mature at his own pace. By his third winter with the team, he was already leading the club in points as well as taking a prominent role in the dressing-room. When Dave Keon left to join the WHA in 1975, Sittler was named team captain and played the finest season of his career. Not only did he set a Leaf record for points, but he was the first Toronto player to reach the 100 mark in a single year. And in this season of seasons, two performances stand out above the rest.

On February 7 of that magical winter, the Leaf captain skated into the NHL spotlight with a performance that has never been matched. In a game against the Boston Bruins, Sittler racked up six goals and four assists for a record total of 10 points. He followed that up in the playoffs, joining Maurice Richard in the record books by firing five goals in a single post-season match. Neither of these marks has been broken, assuring Sittler of a place in the history of the game.

For the next five seasons Sittler played like a champion, averaging over 40 goals and 97 points a year as the Leafs steadily grew in strength and moved up the NHL ladder. Just when it seemed they were ready to vault over the top, their fortunes plummeted. Punch Imlach was brought back as coach in an attempt to rekindle the glory of the 1960s. But Imlach's second coming was a disaster which left the franchise in disarray and Sittler requesting a trade. Much to the dismay of Maple Leaf fans, after 12 years with the Leafs, 6 of them as captain, Sittler was transferred to Philadelphia, ending an era in Toronto.

Sittler's recognition as one of hockey's greats came in 1989 with induction into the Hockey Hall of Fame.

The Toronto Maple Leafs celebrated their 50th anniversary on February 14, 1977. The cover of the 1977 Leaf Fact Book featured four key members of the team who set NHL or Leaf records for 1975–76. Clockwise from top left: Ian Turnbull (20 goals; Leaf record for a defenceman), Borje Salming (57 points; tied Babe Pratt's Leaf record for a defenceman), Lanny McDonald (93 points; Leaf record for a rightwinger), and Darryl Sittler (6 goals and 4 assists in a single game; NHL record).
Maple Leaf Gardens, HHF Archives

Five years into the seventies, the Leafs had still not secured a goaltender of Johnny Bower's stature. Even though Hall of Famers Jacques Plante and Bernie Parent had shared the duties, the team suffered a gap in the last line of defence. Then, in 1976–77, Mike Palmateer established himself as the Leafs' number-one goaltender. Borje Salming was named to the first all-star team, Lanny McDonald skated right wing on the second all-star team, and Ian Turnbull, almost a year to the day of Sittler's big night out, set an NHL record for a defenceman, scoring five goals in a 9–1 Toronto win over Detroit. The lineup was bolstered by draft pick Randy Carlyle and effective role players Pat Boutette and Bob Neely. The Leafs entered the playoffs confident they could recapture their fortunes of earlier years, and, in the quarter-finals against Philadelphia, it appeared they just might succeed.

Lanny McDonald, 1978. "How could I ever forget that goal. The experts had predicted the Islanders to beat us in four or five games, and all of a sudden we were playing in game 7 in overtime. It was a very physical series and Roger Neilson had us not only very well prepared but also believing we could win. I remember Ian Turnbull passing the puck from our blueline to theirs and three guys all close enough to check me but all thinking the other guy would get the job done! When the puck went in it took a few seconds to realize it was all over. It was a tremendous feeling to accomplish something as a team that few people believed we could do."
— Lanny McDonald
Bruce Bennett Studios

Roger Neilson coached the Leafs from 1977 to 1979.
HHF Archival Collection

Toronto won the first two games over the Flyers in Philadelphia and held a convincing two-goal advantage late in the third period of game 3. But the Flyers tied the score in the final minute and won the game in overtime, stemming the tide. The youthful Toronto team could not out-muscle the bullies from Broad Street. Harold Ballard had seen enough of the well-publicized "pyramid power" strategies of Red Kelly, and after this third consecutive playoff loss to Philadelphia, Kelly was relieved of his duties. He was replaced by Roger Neilson, a young coach from the Ontario Hockey League under whose guidance the Leafs would come nearer to the peak of success than they had since the heady days of 1967.

Borje Salming suited up for the Toronto Maple Leafs 1099 times. Only two other men have played more games for the Leafs: George Armstrong (1187) and Tim Horton (1185).

Miles S. Nadal Collection, HHF

Lanny McDonald

When the Toronto Maple Leafs chose Lanny King McDonald as their number-one pick in the 1973 amateur draft, they knew they were getting a solid, front-line player with a good scoring touch. McDonald exceeded all expectations by supplying the anaemic Leaf attack with some well-needed fire power as well as the kind of strength of character that had typified the great Leaf teams of the 1960s.

Having made his mark with the Medicine Hat Tigers of the Western junior league, McDonald arrived in Toronto for the start of the 1973–74 campaign. McDonald's first NHL goal was a game winner against the Montreal Canadiens, proving he had a special gift for scoring in key situations.

In 1975–76 he scored 37 goals, a pace he was to maintain for the rest of his career with the Leafs. Although he followed up that season with three consecutive 40-goal campaigns, it was his heroics in the playoffs that earned Lanny his well-deserved place in the hearts of Leaf fans. During the 1977 post-season, he fired four goals in a game against the Philadelphia Flyers and added a hat trick in a match with the Penguins, becoming the first Leaf to register two hat tricks in the same playoff year. Despite McDonald's milestone performances, the Leafs lost the tough, seven-game series to the Flyers. A year later the Leafs found themselves in a seventh game again, this time with the New York Islanders providing the opposition. McDonald, despite a serious cut near the eye and a broken nose, insisted on suiting up and taking his regular shift. His perseverance paid off for the Leafs when, at the 4:13 mark of sudden-death overtime, he wristed a shot past Chico Resch to send the Leafs to the semi-finals for the first time since 1967.

McDonald's stay in Toronto came to a swift and bitter end when he became the unwilling victim of a power play between Darryl Sittler and Punch Imlach. McDonald was sent packing to the Colorado Rockies. Leaf fans were outraged, and best friend Sittler resigned as captain in protest. McDonald continued to play high-level hockey, both in Denver and later in Calgary, where he scored his five-hundredth goal and registered his thousandth career point. He remains one of the best-loved players ever to wear the Maple Leaf.

The Leafs met the Habs in the 1977–78 semi-finals.
HHF Archival Collection

The 1977–78 Leafs tied a team record for victories, out-scoring their opponents on 41 occasions. Ron Ellis returned to the lineup from retirement and Darryl Sittler racked up 117 points as the Leafs had their best year since 1951. After an opening-series win against Los Angeles, the Leafs met the New York Islanders in the quarter-final round. They fell behind two games but rallied to tie the series, only to see the Islanders win a hard-fought overtime match in game 5. The Leafs come back with a 5–2 win in game 6 and returned to Long Island for the seventh and deciding tilt. Mike Palmateer was outstanding as the teams played though 60 minutes of regulation time. Then, at 4:13 of overtime, Lanny McDonald fired a long wrist shot that eluded the grasp of Chico Resch. The Toronto Maple Leafs had reached the semi-finals for the first time in 11 years. Unfortunately, they ran head first into the powerful Montreal Canadiens who burst the Leafs' bubble in four straight games.

The Leafs traded their first-round draft choices in 1978 and 1980 for the toughness and experience of veteran Dan Maloney. Although his best years were behind him, Maloney was a steady workhorse who led by example. He stayed on to coach after his retirement and proved to be an excellent motivator of young talent.
Miles S. Nadal Collection, HHF

The Leafs tried numerous goalies in the early eighties, but settled on the "Popcorn Kid" as their number one goaltender. Mike Palmateer's acrobatic flair made him a crowd favourite, but he was also a money goalie who saved his best performances for the playoffs when all the cards were on the table.

Miles S. Nadal Collection, HHF

Mike Palmateer

The success of a goaltender cannot always be measured by his career line in the NHL record books. The story of Mike Palmateer is a case in point. In his six seasons and 296 games with the Leafs he managed 15 shutouts and posted a 3.43 goals-against average — respectable but not remarkable. Still, he was one of the few stars of the late-seventies team, an idol of the fans, and a thorn in the side of the opposing team.

The Leafs drafted the "Popcorn Kid" in 1974 and by the 1977 season he was ready to step into the fray as their number-one goaltender. Over the next four winters, Palmateer was the Leafs' workhorse, averaging 52 games a season and always coming out on the credit side of the ledger in wins. On many nights it was the Palmateer magic that led the Leafs to victory. With an acrobatic flair that often infuriated the opposition and charmed the fansl, Palmy back-stopped the Leafs to their greatest success in a decade. In 1977–78 Toronto ousted the Islanders in a series that will long be remembered by Leaf enthusiasts, not so much for the result as for the quality of the hockey it produced. Mike Palmateer was outstanding in this post-season war, shutting down the explosive Islander attack with the performance of a lifetime.

The Leafs shipped Palmateer to Washington in 1980, but retrieved him in 1982. He performed steadily for another two NHL schedules, until a disabling knee injury ended his playing career after the 1983–84 season.

On December 29, 1979, Lanny McDonald, one of the teams most popular players, was traded away. To add insult to injury, the Leafs dealt Lanny to the Colorado Rockies, perennial cellar-dwellers in hockey's oblivion.

Miles S. Nadal Collection, HHF

Many pundits believed that the Leafs were within a couple of players of the Stanley Cup. Their lineup had been carefully nurtured and, like the great Leaf teams of the past, now contained a solid mix of youth and experience. Despite the optimism engendered by the success of the previous spring, cracks began to show in the organization. Coach Roger Neilson had assembled a well-honed defensive unit, but there was one change he wanted to make.

In the spring of 1978, Borje Salming suffered a serious eye injury. His blueline mate, Ian Turnbull, took up the slack and played to unusual advantage. Turnbull's offensive prowess that spring was well documented, but it was Neilson's opinion that Turnbull could not maintain that level of play. Based on his performance in the playoffs, however, Neilson knew that Turnbull's talents were valuable on the open market and approached Ballard with the idea of dealing Turnbull while his stock was still high. This suggestion elicited Ballard's famous "I wouldn't trade Ian Turnbull for God!" and signalled the beginning of the end of Neilson's brief career in Toronto. The Leafs traded Randy Carlyle instead of Turnbull, believing that in Dave Burrows they had obtained a rough defensive specialist. Unfortunately for the Leafs, Burrows talents never materialized, and after three seasons he was sent packing to Pittsburgh.

The 1978–79 season began with great promise but ground to a halt on April 22, 1979, when the Montreal Canadiens swept the Leafs out of the playoffs. As good as the Leafs had been in the 1970s, it staggers the imagination to think of the players they passed over in the amateur drafts, including Mark Howe, Mike Bossy, Bryan Trottier, Rick Middleton, Dennis Maruk, and Pierre Mondou. When these men were on the auction block, the Leaf scouts looked past them to find Don Ashbee, Jack Valiquette, Trevor Johansen, Randy Osburn, and Bob Neely. Add these to the questionable trading of their 1971, 1976, and 1978 first-round draft picks, and the roots of the 1980s "decade of doom" are obvious.

At one time, the Leafs had their own Number 99. The team acquired scrappy Wilf Paiement when they traded Lanny McDonald, and he set a team record for points by a rightwinger in 1980–81, collecting 40 goals and 57 assists.
Miles S. Nadal Collection, HHF

Bill Derlago, who joined the Leafs as part of the Tiger Williams trade, was a superstar from the western junior leagues. He never reached the same level of success in the NHL, but he combined with John Anderson and Rick Vaive to form a potent trio that generated Leaf fortunes in the early 1980s.
Miles S. Nadal Collection, HHF

The key to Rick Vaive's success was his complete lack of fear. He would stand in the crease, taking all kinds of hacks and slashes to score that all-important goal. In 1982 he became the first Leaf to score 50 goals and repeated the performance in 1983 and 1984. Vaive was also expert at drawing the opposition into retaliation penalties, often using the ensuing power-play to pad his expanding goal total.
Miles S. Nadal Collection, HHF

In a scene all too familiar to Leaf fans, this photo pretty well sums up the fortunes of the Leafs in the early 1980s: Salming down, the goalie out of position, and the rest of the team watching as the puck enters the Leaf net.
Miles S. Nadal Collection, HHF

In the 1980s, the Leafs went through nine different coaches and four general managers; they missed the playoffs four times and never finished above the .500 mark, whereas in the previous 50 years, from 1928 to 1979, they had had only 12 coaches and had won 11 Stanley Cups. This alone should serve to indicate that there was rot at the core of one of sport's oldest and proudest franchises. The 1980s will be years to forget in the long march of Maple Leaf history. There are, however, some painful stories that must be told. Following the Leafs' hasty exit from the 1979 playoffs, Harold Ballard dismissed Roger Neilson and general manager Jim Gregory. To Ballard's credit, the men he sought to replace them were Don Cherry and Scotty Bowman, but neither one came. Bowman decided to accept an offer from the Buffalo Sabres where he did double duty as coach and general manager; Don Cherry had already accepted a high-paying post with the Colorado Rockies.

Ballard then looked to an old ally, the miracle worker of the sixties. Punch Imlach would make a comeback. Imlach was still the old drill sergeant, but hockey and hockey players had changed. They now had unions and agents and were in a position to make demands. It was Imlach's inability to adapt to these changes that led to the franchise's downfall. He became vindictive in the face of player defiance and took his revenge by trading away the heart and soul of the team.

Mike Palmateer was dispatched to Washington for somebody named Tim Coulis. Pat Boutette was sent packing to Hartford, but the Leafs received no commensurate return. Ian Turnbull went to Los Angeles (God was not part of the deal). The worst blow for both the Leafs and their fans was the sacking of Lanny McDonald. Lanny was one of the best-loved players the Leafs had ever nurtured, and though he will more likely be remembered for the excellence he later achieved with the Calgary Flames, Toronto fans still claim his as their own. He went west, to hockey's oblivion, Colorado, along with Joel Quenneville in return for Wilf Paiement and Pat Hickey.

Although Punch Imlach's second tenure at the helm of the Toronto Maple Leafs was a failure in most respects, he made one excellent investment for the team's future. He swapped Tiger Williams and Jerry Butler for Rick Vaive and Bill Derlago. The key to the deal was the acquisition of Vaive, who became one of the deadliest snipers on NHL ice and an outspoken leader in the dressing room.
Miles S. Nadal Collection, HHF

Rick Vaive

Punch Imlach's second regime as general manager of the Toronto Maple Leafs (1979–81) was a two-year nightmare for both the team and the individual players. He did, however, make one deal that was little short of a master stroke. On February 18, 1980, he sent fan favourite Tiger Williams roaring off to the West Coast in return for a couple of untried greenhorns, Rick Vaive and Bill Derlago. Although popular opinion was against the move, Vaive's irrefutable talents soon brought the fans around.

Though born in Ottawa, Vaive was raised in the fresh air of Prince Edward Island, where he would practice his shot for hours against the side of the barn. This homey Maritime training technique paid dividends, for the Vaive slapshot would soon put fear into the eyes of opposing goaltenders.

After a stint in junior with Sherbrooke, Vaive was signed to play for the Birmingham "Baby" Bulls of the WHA at the tender age of 18. In the 1979 expansion he was drafted by Vancouver and, in Punch Imlach's last coup, arrived in Toronto soon after. Vaive possessed a rare combination of talents that belied his age: leadership ability, an accurate and explosive slapshot, and the desire to mix it up with all comers. In 1981–82, after being named the youngest captain in the history of the team, Vaive became the first Leaf to score 50 goals in a season, a feat he repeated in the next two campaigns.

Unfortunately, these were lean years for the Leafs, and Vaive never received the respect he undoubtedly would have, had the team played up to his level. After a stormy eight seasons, the Leafs and Vaive parted ways, but his slapshot continues to echo around the NHL.

The Leafs used their first pick in the 1977 amateur draft to select John Anderson, an all-star with the Toronto Marlboros. Anderson started slowly, but when he was teamed with Vaive and Derlago, he became a consistent goal-getter, averaging 30 or more goals for four straight campaigns before being dealt to the Quebec Nordiques.

Miles S. Nadal Collection, HHF

Peter Ihnacak, 1983. After 12 years with the Leafs, Darryl Sittler was traded to the Philadelphia Flyers on January 20, 1982. In return the Leafs acquired Peter Ihnacak, Ken Strong, and Rich Costello. Strong's NHL career lasted only 15 games, while Costello's career was limited to 12 appearances with the Leafs. Ihnacak, who set a Leaf rookie record for points, was released following the 1989–90 season.

Miles S. Nadal Collection, HHF

Wendel Clark

When Wendel Clark made his first sweep of the Gardens rink in 1985, the Leaf faithful seemed to awake from a deep sleep. As a teenager, Clark attended Notre Dame College in Wilcox, Saskatchewan, where he played for the Hounds, a team that has graduated many outstanding players with strong competitive spirit. Clark learned his lessons well and approaches the game with a fervour that has made him the most popular Leaf since the days of Sittler and McDonald. Whether he's steamrolling over opponents or unleashing his whistling wrist shot, Clark does it all with style and ease.

In his rookie campaign (1985–86), Clark had an instant impact—usually on some unsuspecting rival. He made the all-rookie team and was the Leafs' representative at the all-star game. He led the Leafs in scoring with 37 goals the following winter and was chosen to attend the training camp for Team Canada's defence of the Canada Cup. There was no doubt that Clark was the Leafs' best player. Then, during a Team Canada exhibition game, Clark damaged his back, an injury that has greatly reduced his playing time. Despite the constant pain, Clark has not altered his aggressive style of play, and it is likely that NHL opponents will be facing the bone-crunching checks of the "Hound" for years to come.

After missing the playoffs in 1984–85, the Leafs were awarded the first selection overall in the amateur draft. The team needed more than just talent — it needed someone who could inspire the players and revive their flickering hopes. It's doubtful they could have made a wiser choice than Wendel Clark as the number-one selection. Clark wears the Maple Leaf with such spirit that fans can only marvel at his dedication to the game, the city, and the sweater.
Bruce Bennett Studios

Through all of this, Captain Darryl Sittler was the most outspoken critic of the team's mismanagement. He had been the team's spokesman and leading light and as such was the focal point of Imlach's anger. But now his closest teammates were gone, his best friend, Lanny, sent to the worst club in the league, and it didn't seem that there was anything left to fight for.

Shortly after the start of the 1981–82 season, Sittler left the team, demanding to be dealt to another organization.

The stress of his first season back exacted a heavy toll from Imlach. He suffered a heart attack, and returned much weakened for the 1980–81 season. The following summer a second heart attack was followed by by-pass surgery, and although he recovered, he never returned to the Leafs. The erosion of the Leaf franchise was completed on January 20, 1982, when Darryl Sittler was granted his wish and joined the hated Philadelphia Flyers where hockey was still a priority.

Mike Nykoluk, who had taken over the Leaf bench mid-way through the 1980–81 season, lasted only two and a half years. In that time he managed to get the Leafs into the playoffs, but they never made it past the first round. Dan Maloney took a turn at the wheel for the 1983–84 campaign, and in his second year led the team to their best post-season performance of the decade. Though the team lost a tough seven-game quarter-final to St. Louis, their fortunes seemed to be changing. But when Maloney asked for a two-year contract, he was met with grunts and delays at Maple Leaf Gardens, so he took his talents to Winnipeg as coach of the Jets. Maloney's replacement was John Brophy who lasted two and a half years. A few days before Christmas of 1988 Brophy was dismissed. It was left to a reluctant George Armstrong to get the team through the season.

Typical of the misfortunes that plagued the Leafs in the early eighties was the choice of Gary Nylund as their number-one pick in the 1982 draft — he suffered two severe knee injuries before he had a chance to show what he could do in a Leaf jersey. Nylund never fully recovered from these setbacks, and, although he still patrols the blueline in the NHL, he never became the game-breaker the Leafs expected. He was signed as a free agent by Chicago and eventually traded to the Islanders.

Miles S. Nadal Collection, HHF

Gary Leeman

One of the most talented Leafs to alleviate the gloom of the last decade is Gary Leeman. The Leafs drafted Leeman, all-star defenceman and playmaker with the WHL's Regina Pats, with the intention of turning him into a right winger. There was never any doubt of Leeman's athletic abilities, but the transformation from the blueline to the front line was a slow and sometimes frustrating process. He spent parts of his first three NHL winters toiling in the AHL, and it wasn't until he was put on a line with Saskatchewanians Russ Courtnall and Wendel Clark that Leeman's true potential was unleashed.

When coach John Brophy formed the "Hound Line" (Leeman, Courtnall, and Clark had all played for the Hounds at Notre Dame College in Saskatchewan), the benefits were evident immediately. The trio complemented each other with skill, speed, and finesse, and together they brought the team back into prosperity.

Many pundits felt the trade of Courtnall, and Clark's serious back injury, would have adverse effects on Leeman's growth. Instead, Leeman continued to improve. After an excellent 1989 season, he won a spot for the Leafs at the all-star game, where he fired one goal and set up another. As the trigger man on the 1989–90 "GEM" Line, Leeman and fellow jewels Eddie Olcyzk and Mark Osborne have helped the Leafs to their best finish in a decade.

Allan Bester's career in the Toronto net began in 1983. Shortly after making his professional debut, he was blasted with 65 shots in a game against Hartford. The diminutive goalie is still guarding the gate for the Leafs, a testimony to his skill in the game's most precarious position.

Bruce Bennett Studios

Not all was doom and gloom. Wilf Paiement set a Leaf record for most points by a right winger in 1981, piling up 40 goals and 57 assists on the season. Rick Vaive arrived in Toronto as part of the Tiger Williams trade and had three consecutive 50-goal seasons, the first Leaf to ever reach that vaunted mark. His linemate, John Anderson, had four consecutive 30-goal seasons before being traded to Quebec. Peter Ihnacak arrived as part of the Darryl Sittler trade and set a mark for most points by a rookie in one season, with 28 goals and 38 assists. The Leafs had been going through goalies at an alarming rate before settling in with Allan Bester and Ken Wregget in 1983–84. Wendel Clark, the Leafs' first-round choice in 1985, would be a prize for any team. He single-handedly restored the spirit of the team, and in their return toward respectability the Leafs have often ridden on his broad shoulders.

Gary Leeman, an all-star defenceman from the Regina Pats, was a second-round 1982 draft pick. The Leafs transformed Leeman into a power forward. The transition was slow but the Leafs had patience and it paid dividends. Leeman, here wearing Number 4 in his rookie campaign, has become the Leafs most consistent performer. In 1989 he was chosen to represent the team at the all-star game.

Miles S. Nadal Collection, HHF

The 1989–90 Toronto Maple Leafs swarm the Philadelphia Flyers' cage. Led by snipers such as Daniel Marois (Number 32) and playmakers like Tom Fergus (seen turning away from the net, far right), the Leafs became an offensive powerhouse, leading the NHL in goals scored for much of the season.
Doug MacLellan, HHF

Dan Daoust during his rookie campaign in 1982. Dangerous Dan came to the Leafs from the Montreal Canadiens — one of the rare French-Canadian players to suit up for the Leafs.
Miles S. Nadal Collection, HHF

"Gary started out as a defenceman, played a couple of years on and off as a defenceman, and then they moved him to forward. He hasn't looked back since. He's improved point-wise each and every year and he's getting better and better as a forward." — Brad Marsh

Bruce Bennett Studios

On October 3, 1988, the Leafs grabbed Brad Marsh from the Flyers in the NHL waiver draft. A fan favourite, Marsh has never wavered since, becoming a stalwart on the Leaf defence and an inspiration to all the grinders in other NHL arenas.

Bruce Bennett Studios

Lou Franceschetti, a relentless fore-checker who loves to lay on the body, has become a role model for all the Leafs, both young and old. Franceschetti was traded to Toronto by the Washington Capitols.

Bruce Bennett Studios

Al Iafrate, the Leafs' first selection in the 1984 draft, was thrown into the NHL ice-wars at the tender age of 18. He has matured into Toronto's offensive sparkplug from the blueline. Iafrate, seen here in his rookie season with "The Tubmeister," Greg Terrion, and Ken Wregget, has taken control of his game and stands poised to lead the team into the 1990s as an NHL superstar.

Miles S. Nadal Collection, HHF

Al Iafrate

One of the current and rising stars of the Toronto Maple Leafs is Al Iafrate who, at 6-foot-3 and 215 pounds, has all the equipment needed to become a dominant blueliner in the NHL. Following a shining performance with the U.S. Olympic team, Iafrate became the Leafs' number-one choice in the June 1984 draft. After an impressive training-camp display the following September he made the team, but at 19 years of age and with little minor-league experience, he was forced to learn on the job.

Iafrate's first three seasons showed only glimpses of the promise that had been forecast for him, but in 1987 when he began his fourth campaign with the Leafs, a noticeable difference was apparent in his play. Iafrate now handled the puck with assurance and dexterity: he began to take control of the game rather than having it control him. He fired 22 goals that year, tying a Leaf record for a defenceman, and earned an appearance in the 1988 all-star game.

Although Iafrate was plagued by injuries and personal problems in the 1988–89 season, he came back for 1989–90 with a revitalized spirit and enthusiasm. With Iafrate's game back on track the Leafs enjoyed their finest season in a decade. Named to represent his team at the 1990 all-star game, Iafrate turned in an outstanding performance at the all-round skills competition held prior to the game. Big Al outgunned favourite Al MacInnis to win the slapshot event and finished a whisker behind Mike Gartner in the speed skating event. With his style and his explosive slapshot, Al Iafrate seems destined to control the Maple Leaf blueline for years to come.

Ed Olczyk. When the Leafs lost Gary Nylund to free agency in 1986, they wanted Eddie Olczyk as compensation. Though the arbitrating judge disagreed, the Leafs were undaunted in their pursuit of the Chicago native. They traded Rick Vaive to obtain Olczyk and he quickly became a star. His 90 points led the team in 1988–89 and in 1989–90 he tied Darryl Sittler's mark by chalking up at least one point in 18 consecutive games.

Bruce Bennett Studios

"Al has played six years in the league and he's only 24 years old. He's shown great improvement and he's one of the better defencemen in the league now. He's gonna be around for a long time to come and he's gonna break a few records along the way." — Brad Marsh

Bruce Bennett Studios

The end of the decade has seen a return to hope and tradition. The wise use of draft choices — Clark, Iafrate, Damphousse, Marois, Pearson, and McIntyre, the addition of crafty veterans — Ramage, Marsh, Reid, Franceschetti, and Hannan, and the maturing of front-line players — Olczyk, Leeman, the second Leaf to score 50 goals in a season, and Bester — all point to a rejuvenation of spirit on the Toronto Maple Leafs bench. The 1989–90 team surprised critics and fans alike with their goal-scoring prowess. They were the first squad in the league to reach the 300-goal mark; Daniel Marois became one of the NHL's most feared snipers; Vincent Damphousse erased Frank Mahovlich's 29-year-old record of 84 points by a leftwinger; and Gary Leeman and Eddie Olczyk formed one of the most dynamic duos to be seen on Gardens ice in many years.

The most favourable indication of the future is the able manner in which the franchise is being reconstructed. Younger talent is once more being groomed in the minor leagues; Doug Carpenter, who is at his best with struggling young players, is a talented coach. Taking over from the late Harold Ballard in the spring of 1990, the new management, in what is perhaps the most hopeful sign for the Leafs' future, has begun to look at the club's history, in a spirit of pride and respect, for guidance, example, and inspiration.

Miles S. Nadal Collection, HHF

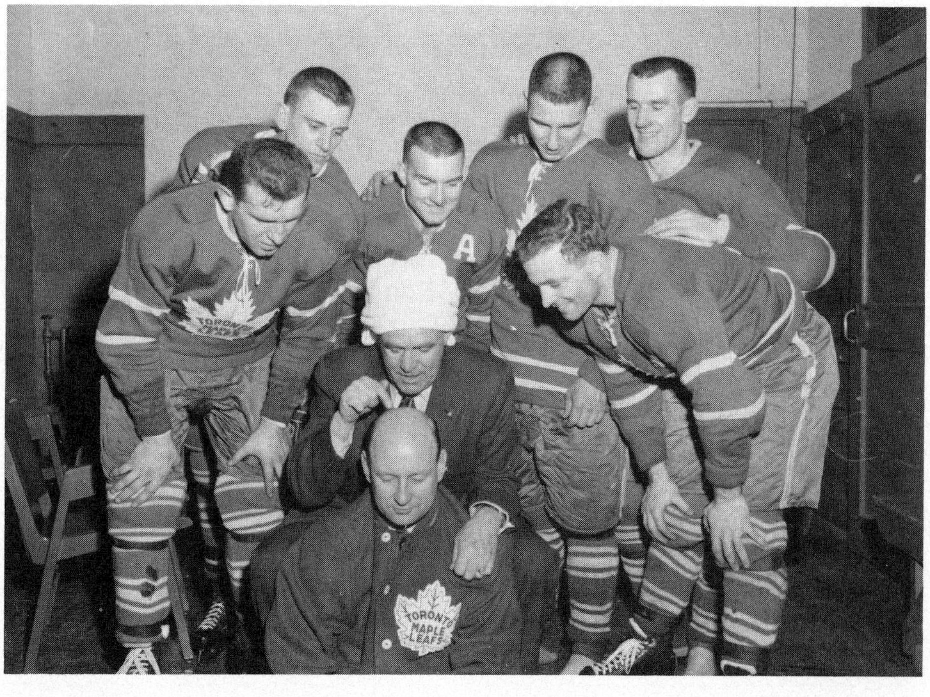

King Clancy peers into Punch Imlach's "crystal ball."
HHF Archival Collection

General Managers

Conn Smythe, 1927–28 to 1957
Hap Day, 1957
Punch Imlach, 1958–59 to 1969
Jim Gregory, 1969 to 1979
Punch Imlach, 1979 to 1981
Gerry McNamara, 1981 to 1988
Gord Stellick, 1988 to 1989
Floyd Smith, 1989 to present

Coaches

Alex Romeril and Conn Smythe, 1927–28 to 1929–30
Conn Smythe and Art Duncan, 1930–31
Art Duncan and Dick Irvin, 1931–32
Dick Irvin, 1932–33 to 1939–40
Hap Day, 1940–41 to 1949–50
Joe Primeau, 1950–51 to 1952–53
"King" Clancy, 1953–54 to 1955–56
Howie Meeker, 1956–57
Billy Reay, 1957–58 to 1958–59
Punch Imlach, 1958–59 to 1968–69
John McLellan, 1969–70 to 1972–73
Leonard "Red" Kelly, 1973–74 to 1976–77
Roger Neilson, 1977–78 to 1978–79
Floyd Smith, 1979–80
Punch Imlach, 1980–81
Joe Crozier, 1980–81
Mike Nykoluk, 1981–82 to 1983–84
Dan Maloney, 1984–85 to 1985–86
John Brophy, 1986–87 to 1987–88
George Armstrong, 1988–89
Doug Carpenter, 1989–90

Statistics compiled by Jack Felstead.

Captains

Hap Day, 1927–28 to 1936–37
Charlie Conacher, 1937–38
Red Horner, 1938–39 to 1939–40
Syl Apps, 1940–41 to 1942–43
Bob Davidson, 1943–44 to 1944–45
Syl Apps, 1945–46 to 1947–48
Ted Kennedy, 1948–49 to 1954–55
Sid Smith, 1955–56
Ted Kennedy and Jim Thomson, 1956–57
George Armstrong, 1957–58 to 1968–69
Dave Keon, 1969–70 to 1974–75
Darryl Sittler, 1975–76 to 1980–81
Rick Vaive, 1981–82 to 1984–85
Rob Ramage, 1989–90

Dave Keon
Frank Prazak Collection, HHF

All-Time Player Roster

Name (Seasons Played)	Pos.	No.	GP	G	A	TP	PIM
Acomb, Doug, 1969–70	C	22	2	0	1	1	0
Adam, Russ, 1982–83	C	16	8	1	2	3	11
Adams, Stewart, 1932–33	LW	9	9	0	2	2	0
Aldcorn, Gary, 1956–57 to 1958–59	LW	21, 22, 26	86	15	18	33	18
Alexander, Claire, 1974–75 to 1976–77	D	20	123	10	29	39	30
Allison, Mike, 1986–87 to 1987–88	LW	8	86	7	19	26	76
Anderson, John, 1977–78 to 1984–85	RW	10, 28	534	189	204	393	168
Apps, Syl, 1936–37 to 1942–43; 1945–46 to 1947–48	C	10	423	201	231	432	56
Arbour, Al, 1961–62 to 1963–64; 1965–66	D	3	66	2	7	9	74
Arbour, Jack, 1928–29	F	2	10	1	0	1	10
Armstrong, George, 1949–50; 1951–52 to 1970–71	RW	10, 15, 20	1187	296	417	713	721
Armstrong, Murray, 1937–38 to 1938–39	C	17	12	0	1	1	0
Armstrong, Norm, 1962–63	D	18	7	1	1	2	2
Armstrong, Tim, 1988–89	C	8	11	1	0	1	6
Arundel, John, 1949–50	D	25	3	0	0	0	9
Ashby, Don, 1975–76 to 1978–79	C	9, 20	141	26	40	66	34
Aubin, Normand, 1981–82 to 1982–83	C	24, 35	69	18	13	31	30
Backor, Peter, 1944–45	D	14	36	4	5	9	6
Bailey, Irvine (Ace), 1926–27 to 1933–34	LW	6, 12, 8	313	111	82	193	472
Bailey, Bob, 1953–54 to 1955–56	RW	17, 18, 20, 21, 23	86	6	9	15	128
Bailey, Reid, 1982–83	D	4	1	0	0	0	2
Baldwin, Doug, 1945–46	D	19	15	0	1	1	6
Balfour, Earl, 1951–52; 1953–54; 1955–56; 1957–58	LW	16, 22, 24, 25	80	14	6	20	48
Barbe, Andre, 1950–51	RW	25	1	0	0	0	2
Barilko, Bill, 1946–47 to 1950–51	D	5, 19, 21	252	26	36	62	456
Bathgate, Andy, 1963–64 to 1964–65	RW	9	70	19	44	63	42
Baun, Bob, 1956–57 to 1966–67; 1970–71 to 1972–73	D	21, 26	739	29	140	169	1155
Belanger, Alain, 1977–78	RW	17	9	0	1	1	6
Bellefeuille, Peter, 1926–27	RW	10	13	0	0	0	12
Benning, Jim, 1981–82 to 1986–87	D	3, 15	364	37	136	173	289
Bentley, Max, 1947–48 to 1952–53	C	7	354	122	134	256	136
Bionda, Jack, 1955–56	D	22	13	0	1	1	18
Blair, Andy, 1928–29 to 1935–36	C	5, 12	361	74	83	157	290
Blair, Charles, 1948–49	RW	22	1	0	0	0	0
Blair, George (Dusty), 1950–51	C	14	2	0	0	0	0
Blaisdell, Mike, 1987–88 to 1988–89	RW	22	27	4	2	6	6
Blake, Mickey, 1935–36	D	3	8	0	0	0	2
Bodnar, Gus, 1943–44 to 1946–47	C	8, 21	187	48	105	153	60
Boesch, Garth, 1946–47 to 1949–50	D	5, 18	197	9	28	37	205
Boimistruck, Fred, 1981–82 to 1982–83	D	11	83	4	14	18	45
Boisvert, Serge, 1982–83	RW	12	17	0	2	2	4
Boivin, Leo, 1951–52 to 1954–55	D	16, 18, 19, 21	137	3	20	23	186
Boll, Frank (Buzz), 1933–34 to 1938–39	LW	8, 17	213	61	39	100	69
Bolton, Hugh, 1949–50 to 1956–57	D	4, 19, 23	235	10	51	61	221
Boothman, George, 1942–43 to 1943–44	RW	14, 16	58	17	19	36	18
Boschman, Laurie, 1979–80 to 1981–82	C	12	187	39	70	109	406
Boudreau, Bruce, 1976–77 to 1982–83	C	12, 19, 35, 11, 17	134	27	42	69	44
Bourgault, Leo, 1926–27	D	6	22	0	0	0	44
Boutette, Pat, 1975–76 to 1979–80	RW	15	349	59	82	141	520

All-Time Player Roster — *continued*

Name (Seasons Played)	Pos.	No.	GP	G	A	TP	PIM
Boyer, Wally, 1965–66	C	15	46	4	17	21	23
Brenneman, John, 1966–67	LW	24	41	6	4	10	4
Brewer, Carl, 1957–58 to 1964–65; 1979–80	D	2, 18, 28	473	19	136	155	917
Brindley, Doug, 1970–71	C	17	3	0	0	0	0
Britz, Greg, 1983–84 to 1984–85	RW	16, 32	7	0	0	0	4
Brossart, Willie, 1973–74 to 1974–75	D	25	21	0	1	1	22
Brown, Arnie, 1961–62; 1963–64	D	16, 22	6	0	0	0	6
Brubaker, Jeff, 1984–85 to 1985–86	LW	23	89	8	4	12	276
Brydge, Bill, 1926–27	D	3	41	6	3	9	76
Brydson, Gord, 1929–30	F	12	8	2	0	2	8
Buchanan, Bill, 1948–49 to 1949–50	LW	24, 25	4	0	1	1	2
Burega, Bill, 1955–56	D	20	4	0	1	1	4
Burrows, Dave, 1978–79 to 1980–81	D	26	151	5	27	32	72
Butler, Jerry, 1977–78 to 1979–80	RW	17	204	24	22	46	130
Byers, Mike, 1967–68 to 1968–69	RW	24	15	2	2	4	2
Caffery, Jack, 1954–55	C	25	3	0	0	0	0
Cahan, Larry, 1954–55 to 1955–56	D	20	79	0	8	8	110
Capuano, Jack, 1989–90	D	26	1	0	0	0	0
Carleton, Wayne, 1965–66 to 1969–70	LW	25	91	10	16	26	60
Carlyle, Randy, 1976–77 to 1977–78	D	23, 28	94	2	16	18	82
Carr, Red, 1943–44	LW	14	5	0	1	1	4
Carr, Lorne, 1941–42 to 1945–46	RW	9	236	105	121	226	37
Carriere, Larry, 1979–80	D	3	2	0	1	1	0
Carson, William, 1926–27 to 1928–29	F	15	96	43	18	61	122
Ceresino, Ray, 1948–49	F	16	12	1	1	2	2
Chamberlain, Murph, 1937–38 to 1939–40	C/LW	8, 14	131	19	45	64	146
Champagne, Andre, 1962–63	LW		2	0	0	0	0
Chisholm, Lex, 1939–40 to 1940–41	C	9, 22	54	10	8	18	19
Church, Jack, 1938–39 to 1941–42	D	16	72	1	11	12	114
Clancy, King, 1930–31 to 1936–37	D	7, 5	286	52	78	130	383
Clancy, Terry, 1968–69 to 1969–70; 1972–73	RW	7, 21	86	6	6	12	37
Clark, Wendel, 1985–86 to 1989–90	LW	17	227	108	57	165	760
Collins, Gary, 1958–59	C	24	2	0	0	0	0
Conacher, Brian, 1961–62; 1965–66 to 1967–68	LW	17, 22	133	25	27	52	80
Conacher, Charlie, 1929–30 to 1937–38	RW	9, 6	326	200	124	324	414
Conacher, Pete, 1957–58	LW	16	5	0	1	1	5
Copp, Robert, 1942–43; 1950–51	D	2	40	3	9	12	26
Corbeau, Bert, 1926–27	D	2	41	1	2	3	88
Corrigan, Charlie, 1937–38	RW	19	3	0	0	0	0
Costello, Les, 1948–49	LW	15	15	2	3	5	11
Costello, Rich, 1983–84; 1985–86	C	8, 16	12	2	2	4	2
Cotton, Harold, 1928–29 to 1934–35	LW	8, 11	285	68	88	156	252
Courtnall, Russ, 1983–84 to 1988–89	C	9, 16, 26	309	90	128	218	243
Cox, Dan, 1926–27 to 1929–30	LW	7	116	22	19	41	63
Creighton, Dave, 1954–55; 1958–59 to 1959–60	C	11, 22, 23	62	6	15	21	16
Crozier, Joe, 1959–60	D	23	5	0	3	3	2
Cullen, Barry, 1955–56 to 1958–59	RW	19	164	28	43	71	88
Cullen, Brian, 1954–55 to 1958–59	C	14, 18, 22, 27	220	37	60	97	80
Curran, Brian, 1987–88 to 1989–90	D	28	126	3	14	17	505
Dallman, Marty, 1987–88	C	35, 15	6	0	1	1	0
Damphousse, Vincent, 1986–87 to 1989–90	C/LW	10	315	92	164	256	197
Daoust, Dan, 1982–83 to 1989–90	C	24	518	87	166	253	471
Darragh, Harold, 1931–32 to 1932–33	F	16	57	6	12	18	6
Davidson, Bob, 1934–35 to 1945–46	RW	4, 5, 17, 18	491	94	160	254	398
Davis, Kim, 1980–81	C		2	0	0	0	4
Dawes, Bob, 1946–47, 1948–49 to 1949–50	D	21, 23, 25	17	2	2	4	2
Day, Hap, 1927–27 to 1936–37	D	4, 3	476	62	99	161	528
DeGray, Dale, 1987–88	D	3	56	6	18	24	63
Demarco, Ab, 1942–43	C	17	4	0	1	1	0
Denneny, Corbett, 1926–27	LW	5	29	7	1	8	24
Derlago, Bill, 1979–80 to 1985–86	C	19	378	158	176	334	179
Dickens, Ernie, 1941–42; 1945–46	D	16, 23	25	3	5	8	12
Domi, Tie, 1989–90	RW	40	2	0	0	0	42
Doraty, Ken, 1932–33 to 1934–35	F	15	83	15	25	40	22
Dorey, Jim, 1968–69 to 1971–72	D	8	231	25	74	99	553
Douglas, Kent, 1962–63 to 1966–67	D	19	283	20	65	85	408

All-Time Player Roster — *continued*

Name (Seasons Played)	Pos.	No.	GP	G	A	TP	PIM
Downie, David, 1932–33	C	11	11	0	1	1	2
Draper, Bruce, 1962–63	F		1	0	0	0	0
Drillon, Gord, 1936–37 to 1941–42	LW	12	262	127	117	244	42
Duff, Dick, 1954–55 to 1963–64	LW	9, 17	582	174	165	339	535
Duncan, Art, 1927–28 to 1930–31	D	4	122	15	14	29	199
Dundas, Rocky, 1989–90	LW	34	5	0	0	0	14
Dunlap, Frank, 1943–44	D	20	15	0	1	1	2
Dunn, Dave, 1974–75 to 1975–76	D/F	4	115	3	19	22	226
Dupere, Denis, 1970–71 to 1973–74	LW	17	192	29	44	73	26
Dupont, Jerome, 1986–87	D	2	13	0	0	0	23
Duris, Vitezslav, 1980–81; 1982–83	D	23, 24	89	3	20	23	62
Dye, Babe, 1930–31	RW	14	6	0	0	0	0
Ecclestone, Tim, 1973–74 to 1974–75	LW	16	51	10	15	25	32
Edmundson, Garry (Duke), 1959–60 to 1960–61	LW	25	42	4	6	10	47
Ehman, Gerry, 1958–59 to 1960–61; 1963–64	RW	8, 17	123	26	31	57	40
Ellis, Ron, 1963–64 to 1974–75; 1977–78 to 1980–81	RW	6, 8, 11	1034	332	308	640	207
Erickson, Aut, 1967 (playoffs only)	D	24	1	0	0	0	2
Evans, Chris, 1969–70	D		2	0	0	0	0
Evans, Daryl, 1986–87 to 1988–89	LW	3	2	1	0	1	0
Evans, Paul, 1976–77 to 1977–78	C	17, 28, 29	11	1	1	2	21
Ezinicki, Bill, 1944–45 to 1949–50	RW	12, 16, 17	271	56	79	135	525
Farrish, Dave, 1979–80 to 1980–81; 1982–83 to 1983–84	D	23, 28	209	11	69	80	215
Faulker, Alex, 1961–62	C	8	1	0	0	0	0
Fauss, Ted, 1986–87 to 1988–89	D	2	28	0	2	2	15
Fergus, Tom, 1985–86 to 1989–90	C	19	332	112	172	284	312
Ferguson, George, 1972–73 to 1977–78	C	10	359	57	110	167	236
Finnigan, Frank, 1931–32; 1934–35 to 1936–37	RW	12	154	14	26	40	61
Flaman, Fernie, 1950–51 to 1953–54	D	3, 12	228	4	27	31	368
Flett, Bill, 1974–75	RW	19	77	15	25	40	38
Foley, Gerry, 1954–55	RW	11	4	0	0	0	8
Forsey, Jack, 1942–43	F	17	19	7	9	16	10
Fortier, Dave, 1972–73	D	22	23	1	4	5	63
Fowler, Jim, 1936–37 to 1938–39	D	3	135	18	29	47	39
Franceschetti, Lou, 1989–90	LW	15	80	21	15	36	127
Fryer, Miroslav, 1981–82 to 1987–88	RW	14	328	114	153	267	374
Gagne, Paul, 1988–89	LW	18, 41	16	3	2	5	6
Gamble, Dick, 1965–66 to 1966–67	LW		3	1	0	1	0
Gardner, Cal, 1948–49 to 1951–52	C	17	219	58	95	153	129
Gardner, Paul, 1978–79 to 1979–80	C	18	56	18	15	33	10
Gariepy, Ray, 1955–56	D		1	0	0	0	4
Garland, Scott, 1975–76 to 1976–77	C	25	85	13	23	36	91
Gavin, Stewart, 1980–81 to 1984–85	LW	9, 17	268	34	48	82	214
Gibson, John, 1981–82	D	23	27	0	2	2	67
Gill, Todd, 1984–85 to 1989–90	D	11, 23, 3	258	26	74	100	428
Gingras, Gaston, 1982–83 to 1984–85	D	11	109	17	40	57	26
Girard, Ken, 1956–57 to 1957–58; 1959–60	RW	27	7	0	1	1	2
Glennie, Brian, 1969–70 to 1977–78	D	24	554	12	98	110	599
Godden, Ernie, 1981–82	C	18	5	1	1	2	6
Goldham, Bob, 1941–42; 1945–46 to 1946–47	D	2, 14, 17	79	12	22	34	79
Goldup, Hank, 1939–40 to 1942–43	LW	20, 23	99	29	34	63	28
Gorman, Ed, 1927–28	D		19	0	1	1	30
Gracie, Bob, 1930–31 to 1932–33	LW	14	104	26	23	49	60
Graham, Pat, 1983–84	LW	23	41	4	4	8	65
Gray, Alex, 1928–29	RW	9	7	0	0	0	2
Grisdale, John, 1972–73; 1974–75	D	3	51	1	7	8	80
Gross, Lloyd, 1926–27	LW		16	1	1	2	0
Halderson, Harold, 1926–27	D	14	26	1	2	3	36
Hamel, Hap, 1930–31	F		2	0	0	0	14
Hamilton, Jack, 1942–43 to 1943–44; 1945–46	C	15, 19, 22	138	31	48	79	76
Hamilton, Reg, 1936–37 to 1944–45	D	3, 5	329	17	61	78	379
Hammarstrom, Inge, 1973–74 to 1977–78	LW	11	292	85	82	167	80
Hammond, Ken, 1988–89	D	29	14	0	2	2	12
Hampson, Ted, 1959–60	C	14	41	2	8	10	17
Hannan, Dave, 1989–90	RW	9	39	6	9	15	55

All-Time Player Roster — *continued*

Name (Seasons Played)	Pos.	No.	GP	G	A	TP	PIM
Hannigan, Gord, 1952–53 to 1955–56	C	17, 22, 23	164	29	31	60	117
Hannigan, Pat, 1959–60	RW	23	1	0	0	0	0
Hannigan, Ray, 1948–49	F	16	3	0	0	0	2
Harris, Billy, 1955–56 to 1964–65	C	15	610	106	181	287	187
Harris, Billy, 1981–82 to 1983–84	RW	16	146	20	29	49	44
Harris, Duke, 1967–68	RW		4	0	0	0	0
Harrison, Jim, 1969–70 to 1971–72	C	7, 12	175	39	47	86	248
Hassard, Bob, 1949–50 to 1950–51; 1952–53 to 1953–54	C	17, 20, 25	109	9	28	37	18
Henderson, Paul, 1967–68 to 1973–74	LW	19	408	162	157	319	166
Herberts, Jim, 1927–28	F	7	43	15	4	19	64
Heron, Bob (Red), 1938–39 to 1940–41	C	16, 17, 18	83	20	17	37	24
Hickey, Pat, 1979–80 to 1981–82	LW	15, 16	118	38	49	87	65
Higgins, Paul, 1981–82 to 1982–83	RW	17	25	0	0	0	152
Hill, Mel, 1942–43 to 1945–46	RW	8	146	49	61	110	77
Hillman, Larry, 1960–61 to 1967–68	D	2, 16, 22	277	13	75	88	185
Hinse, Andre, 1967–68	LW		4	0	0	0	0
Hodgson, Dan, 1985–86	C	16	40	13	12	25	12
Hollett, Flash, 1933–34 to 1935–36	D	34	63	11	20	31	50
Hopkins, Larry, 1977–78	LW		2	0	0	0	0
Horne, George, 1928–29	F	8	39	9	3	12	32
Horner, Red, 1928–29 to 1939–40	D	2	490	42	110	152	1264
Horton, Tim, 1949–50; 1951–52 to 1969–70	D	7, 16, 20	1185	109	349	458	1389
Horvath, Bronco, 1962–63	C	17	9	0	4	4	12
Hotham, Greg, 1979–80 to 1981–82	D	4	60	4	11	15	21
Howard, Jack, 1936–37	D	21	2	0	0	0	0
Howe, Syd, 1931–32	C	3	3	0	0	0	0
Huard, Roland, 1930–31	F	15	1	1	0	1	0
Hubick, Greg, 1975–76	F	19	72	6	8	14	10
Hurst, Ron, 1955–56 to 1956–57	RW	21, 22	64	9	7	16	70
Hutchison, Dave, 1978–79 to 1979–80; 1983–84	D	23, 33	157	5	24	29	400
Iafrate, Al, 1984–85 to 1989–90	D	33	430	78	154	232	433
Ihnacak, Miroslav, 1985–86 to 1988–89	LW	27	55	8	9	17	39
Ihnacak, Peter, 1982–83 to 1989–90	C	18, 15	417	102	165	267	175
Imlach, Brent, 1965–66 to 1966–67	F	9, 24	3	0	0	0	2
Ingoldsby, Jack, 1942–43 to 1943–44	RW	11	29	5	1	6	15
Jackson, Art, 1934–35 to 1936–37; 1944–45	C	16, 18, 20	113	17	31	48	26
Jackson, Harvey (Busher), 1929–30 to 1938–39	LW	11, 9	434	186	165	351	342
Jackson, Jeff, 1984–85 to 1986–87	LW	12, 25	77	9	10	19	90
James, Gerry, 1954–55 to 1957–58; 1959–60	RW	11, 16, 19	149	14	26	40	257
James, Val, 1986–87	LW	28	4	0	0	0	14
Jarrett, Gary, 1960–61	LW		1	0	0	0	0
Jarry, Pierre, 1971–72 to 1973–74	LW	8	103	24	30	54	65
Jarvis, Bud, 1936–37	LW	17	24	1	0	1	0
Jarvis, Wes, 1984–85 to 1985–86	C	12, 34, 16	29	1	1	2	4
Jeffrey, Larry, 1965–66 to 1966–67	LW	15, 22	76	12	18	30	49
Jenkins, Roger, 1930–31	D	10	21	0	0	0	12
Johansen, Trevor, 1977–78 to 1978–79; 1981–82	D	2, 4	132	4	21	25	134
Johnson, Danny, 1969–70	C	22	1	0	0	0	0
Johnson, Terry, 1986–87	D	20	48	0	1	1	104
Johnson, William, 1949–50	C		1	0	0	0	0
Johnstone, Ross, 1943–44 to 1944–45	D	12	42	5	4	9	14
Jones, Buck, 1942–43	D	14	16	0	0	0	22
Jones, Jim, 1977–78 to 1979–80	C	16	148	13	18	31	68
Joyal, Ed, 1965–66	C	24	14	0	2	2	2
Juzda, Bill, 1948–49 to 1951–52	D	18	211	3	29	32	175
Kampman, Bingo, 1937–38 to 1941–42	D	7, 17, 20	189	14	30	44	287
Kaszycki, Mike, 1979–80 to 1980–81; 1982–83	C	14, 16	53	5	19	24	22
Keeling, Butch, 1926–27 to 1927–28	LW	10	73	21	8	29	81
Keenan, Larry, 1961–62	LW	8	2	0	0	0	0
Kehoe, Rick, 1971–72 to 1973–74	RW	16, 17	184	59	72	131	32
Kelly, Red, 1959–60 to 1966–67	C	4	470	119	232	351	74
Kelly, Pep, 1934–35 to 1939–40	F	9, 15, 16	230	55	46	101	98
Kemp, Stanley, 1948–49	D		1	0	0	0	2
Kendall, William, 1936–37	F	24	15	2	4	6	4
Kennedy, Forbes, 1968–69	C	22	13	0	3	3	24

All-Time Player Roster — *continued*

Name (Seasons Played)	Pos.	No.	GP	G	A	TP	PIM
Kennedy, Ted, 1942–43 to 1954–55; 1956–57	C	9, 10	696	231	329	560	432
Keon, Dave, 1960–61 to 1974–75	C	14	1062	365	493	858	75
Kilrea, Hec, 1933–34 to 1934–35	LW	12	89	21	26	47	31
Kirton, Mark, 1979–80 to 1980–81	C	20	13	1	0	1	2
Kitchen, Bill, 1984–85	D	26	29	1	4	5	27
Klukay, Joe, 1946–47 to 1951–52; 1954–55 to 1955–56	LW	8, 17, 19	416	72	86	158	130
Knox, Paul, 1954–55	RW		1	0	0	0	0
Kordic, John, 1988–89 to 1989–90	RW	27	101	10	6	16	437
Korn, Jim, 1981–82 to 1984–85	D/LW	20	197	26	43	69	708
Kotsopoulos, Chris, 1985–86 to 1988–89	D	26	182	11	37	48	221
Kozak, Les, 1961–62	F	8	12	1	0	1	2
Kraftcheck, Steve, 1958–59	D	4	8	1	0	1	0
Kurtenbach, Orland, 1965–66	C	25	70	9	6	15	54
Kurvers, Tom, 1989–90	D	25	70	15	37	52	29
Landon, Larry, 1984–85	RW	11	7	0	0	0	2
Langelle, Peter, 1938–39 to 1941–42	C	8, 21	137	22	51	73	11
Lanz, Rick, 1986–87 to 1988–89	D	4	151	9	50	59	115
Laughlin, Craig, 1988–89	RW	14, 18	66	10	13	23	41
Lawless, Paul, 1988–89	RW	20	7	0	0	0	0
Laxdal, Derek, 1986–87 to 1988–89	RW	28, 35	48	9	6	15	78
Leeman, Gary, 1983 playoffs, 1983–84 to 1989–90	RW/D	4, 11	459	152	206	358	380
Levinsky, Alex, 1930–31 to 1933–34	D	3	150	15	28	43	130
Lewicki, Danny, 1950–51 to 1953–54	LW	21	123	21	31	52	66
Ley, Rick, 1968–69 to 1971–72	D	2, 26	229	8	54	62	416
Liddington, Bob, 1970–71	LW	26	11	0	1	1	2
Litzenberger, Ed, 1961–62 to 1963–64	RW	25	114	17	23	40	24
Lowrey, Gerald, 1927–28 to 1928–29	LW	9	53	9	14	23	53
Luce, Don, 1981–82	C	20	39	4	4	8	32
Lundrigan, Joe, 1972–73	D	2	49	2	8	10	20
Lynn, Vic, 1946–47 to 1949–50	LW	14	213	32	58	90	169
MacDonald, Parker, 1952–53; 1954–55	LW	21	63	8	3	11	36
MacKasey, Blair, 1976–77	D	16	1	0	0	0	2
MacKell, Fleming, 1947–48 to 1951–52	C	16	152	22	35	57	58
MacMillan, Bill, 1970–71 to 1971–72	RW	12, 23	137	32	26	58	81
MacMillan, John, 1960–61 to 1963–64	RW	8, 24, 25	82	5	6	11	32
MacNeil, Al, 1955–56 to 1957–58; 1959–60	D	11, 22, 24	71	4	8	12	97
Maggs, Darryl, 1979–80	D	24	5	0	0	0	0
Magnan, Marc, 1982–83	LW	35	4	0	1	1	5
Maguire, Kevin, 1986–87	RW	28	17	0	0	0	74
Mahovlich, Frank, 1956–57 to 1967–68	LW	22, 26, 27	720	296	301	597	782
Maloney, Dan, 1977–78 to 1981–82	LW	9	270	65	84	149	538
Maloney, Phil, 1950–51; 1952–53	C	25	30	3	6	9	2
Mann, Norm, 1938–39; 1940–41	RW	8	31	0	3	3	4
Manno, Bob, 1981–82	D	3, 18	72	9	41	50	67
Marcetta, Milan, 1967 (playoffs only)	C	25	3	0	0	0	0
Marchinko, Brian, 1970–71 to 1971–72	C	22	5	0	0	0	0
Marker, Gus, 1938–39 to 1940–41	RW	14, 18	112	23	20	43	39
Markle, Jack, 1935–36	F	21	8	0	1	1	0
Marois, Daniel, 1988–89 to 1989–90	RW	32	144	70	60	130	158
Marsh, Brad, 1988–89 to 1989–90	D	3	159	2	28	30	174
Marsh, Gary, 1968–69	LW	18	1	0	0	0	0
Marshall, Don, 1971–72	LW	22	50	2	14	16	0
Marshall, Paul, 1980–81 to 1981–82	LW	28	23	2	4	6	4
Marshall, Willie, 1954–55 to 1955–56; 1958–59	C	8, 21, 24	31	1	15	16	2
Martin, Jack, 1960–61	F		1	0	0	0	0
Martin, Terry, 1979–80 to 1983–84	LW	25	317	83	76	159	152
Martin, Tom, 1967–68	RW	17	3	1	0	1	0
Masnick, Paul, 1957–58	C	8	41	2	9	11	14
Mathers, Frank, 1948–49 to 1949–50; 1951–52	D	20	23	1	3	4	4
Maxwell, Brad, 1985–86	D	4	52	8	18	26	108
Maxwell, Wally, 1952–53	F	26	2	0	0	0	0
Mayer, Shep, 1942–43	F	22	12	1	2	3	4
McAdam, Gary, 1985–86	LW	12	15	1	6	7	0
McBride, Roy, 1929–30	D		1	0	0	0	0
McCaffrey, Bert, 1926–27 to 1927–28	D	7	51	6	6	12	52
McCormack, John, 1947–48 to 1950–51	C	20	84	12	13	25	2

All-Time Player Roster — *continued*

Name (Seasons Played)	Pos.	No.	GP	G	A	TP	PIM
McCourt, Dale, 1983–84	C	12	72	19	24	43	10
McCreary, Bill, 1980–81	RW	28	12	1	0	1	4
McCreedy, John, 1941–42; 1944–45	RW	14	64	17	12	29	25
McCutcheon, Darwin, 1981–82	D	2	1	0	0	0	2
McDonald, Bucko, 1938–39 to 1943–44	D	3, 19	195	17	53	70	116
McDonald, Lanny, 1973–74 to 1979–80	RW	7	477	219	240	459	372
McGill, Bob, 1981–82 to 1988–89	D	4, 15	298	3	25	28	954
McIntyre, John, 1989–90	C	44	59	5	12	17	117
McIntyre, Larry, 1969–70; 1972–73	D	25	41	0	3	3	26
McKechnie, Walt, 1978–79 to 1979–80	C	11	133	32	72	104	22
McKenna, Sean, 1987–88 to 1989–90	RW	8	48	5	6	11	32
McKenney, Don, 1963–64 to 1964–65	C	17	67	15	30	45	8
McKenny, Jim, 1965–66 to 1977–78	D	18, 25	594	81	246	327	292
McLean, Jack, 1942–43 to 1944–45	C	7, 18	67	14	24	38	76
McLellan, John, 1951–52	C	14	2	0	0	0	0
McRae, Basil, 1983–84 to 1984–85	LW	26	4	0	0	0	19
McRae, Chris, 1987–88 to 1988–89	LW	32, 29	14	0	0	0	77
Meehan, Gerry, 1968–69	C	26, 27	25	0	2	2	2
Meeker, Howie, 1946–47 to 1953–54	RW	11, 15	346	83	102	185	329
Melrose, Barry, 1980–81 to 1982–83	D	26	173	5	15	20	420
Metz, Don, 1939–40 to 1941–42; 1945–46 to 1948–49	RW	11, 15, 18	172	20	35	55	42
Metz, Nick, 1934–35 to 1941–42; 1944–45 to 1947–48	LW	5, 15, 16, 17	518	131	119	250	149
Mickey, Larry, 1968–69	RW	12	55	8	19	27	43
Migay, Rudy, 1949–50; 1951–52 to 1959–60	C	11, 14, 22	418	59	92	151	293
Mikol, Jim, 1962–63	D	16	4	0	1	1	2
Miller, Earl, 1931–32	F	15	15	3	3	6	10
Moffat, Lyle, 1972–73; 1974–75	LW	26	23	2	7	9	13
Monahan, Gary, 1970–71 to 1974–75; 1978–79	LW	14, 20	375	55	80	135	274
Moore, Dick, 1964–65	RW	16	38	2	4	6	68
Morris, Moe, 1943–44 to 1945–46	D	5	117	13	28	41	50
Morrison, Jim, 1951–52 to 1957–58	D	3, 14, 21, 22, 24	399	25	85	110	358
Mortson, Gus, 1946–47 to 1951–52	D	3, 19	371	21	71	92	669
Mulhern, Richard, 1979–80	D	8	26	0	10	10	11
Muni, Craig, 1981–82 to 1982–83; 1984–85 to 1985–86	D	32, 33	19	0	2	2	6
Murray, Ken, 1969–70 to 1970–71	D	3, 7	5	0	1	1	2
Murray, Randy, 1969–70	D		3	0	0	0	2
Neely, Bob, 1973–74 to 1977–78	D	3	261	36	53	89	264
Nelson, Gord, 1969–70	D	27	3	0	0	0	11
Nesterenko, Eric, 1951–52 to 1955–56	RW	16, 19, 25	206	43	36	79	261
Nevin, Bob, 1957–58 to 1958–59; 1960–61 to 1963–64	RW	11	250	55	100	155	55
Nighbour, Frank, 1929–30	C	7	22	2	0	2	2
Nigro, Frank, 1982–83 to 1983–84	C	32	68	8	18	26	39
Nykoluk, Mike, 1956–57	RW	24, 27	32	3	1	4	20
Nylund, Gary, 1982–83 to 1985–86	D	2	218	7	50	57	398
O'Flaherty, Gerry, 1971–72	LW		2	0	0	0	0
Olczyk, Ed, 1987–88 to 1989–90	LW	16	239	112	141	253	208
Oliver, Murray, 1967–68 to 1969–70	C	11	226	44	90	134	50
Olmstead, Bert, 1958–59 to 1961–62	LW	16	246	56	109	165	231
O'Neill, Windy (Tom), 1943–44 to 1944–45	RW	18	66	10	12	22	53
Osborne, Mark, 1986–87 to 1989–90	LW	12	248	67	127	194	317
Osburn, Randy, 1972–73	LW	16	26	0	2	2	0
Paiement, Wilf, 1979–80 to 1981–82	RW	99	187	78	125	203	420
Pappin, Jim, 1963–64 to 1967–68	RW	17, 18	223	54	46	100	200
Parise, Jean Paul, 1967–68	LW	17	1	0	1	1	0
Parsons, George, 1936–37 to 1938–39	LW	16, 18	64	12	13	25	17
Patterson, George, 1926–27 to 1927–28	RW	6	29	5	2	7	34
Pearson, Scott, 1988–89 to 1989–90	LW	18	50	5	11	16	92
Pelyk, Mike, 1967–68 to 1973–74; 1976–77 to 1977–78	D	4, 21	440	26	88	114	566
Perlini, Fred, 1981–82; 1983–84	C	8, 28, 29	8	2	3	5	0
Pettinger, Eric, 1928–29 to 1929–30	LW	10	68	7	12	19	64
Picard, Robert, 1980–81	D	4	59	6	19	25	68
Pilote, Pierre, 1968–69	D	2	69	3	18	21	46
Plante, Cam, 1984–85	D	11	2	0	0	0	0
Poddubny, Walt, 1981–82 to 1985–86	LW	8, 12	186	59	86	145	178

All-Time Player Roster — *continued*

Name (Seasons Played)	Pos.	No.	GP	G	A	TP	PIM
Poile, Norman (Bud), 1942–43 to 1943–44; 1945–46 to 1947–48	C	7, 11, 16, 25	131	44	52	96	52
Pratt, Tracy, 1976–77	D	4	11	0	1	1	8
Pratt, Walter (Babe), 1942–43 to 1945–46	D	2, 12	181	52	108	160	149
Prentice, Eric, 1943–44	D	17	5	0	0	0	4
Price, Noel, 1957–58 to 1958–59	D	23	29	0	0	0	9
Primeau, Joe, 1927–28 to 1935–36	C	10, 7	310	66	177	243	111
Pronovost, Marcel, 1965–66 to 1969–70	D	3	223	8	40	48	134
Pudas, Albert, 1926–27	LW		3	0	0	0	0
Pulford, Bob, 1956–57 to 1969–70	C	20	947	251	312	563	691
Quenneville, Joel, 1978–79 to 1979–80	D	3	93	3	13	16	84
Quinn, Pat, 1968–69 to 1969–70	D	23	99	2	12	14	183
Ramage, Rob, 1989–90	D	8	80	8	41	49	202
Ramsey, Beattie, 1927–28	D	2	43	0	2	2	10
Reaume, Marc, 1954–55 to 1959–60	D	2, 25	270	8	39	47	247
Regan, Larry, 1958–59 to 1960–61	RW	8	116	11	42	53	10
Reid, David, 1952–53; 1954–55 to 1955–56	F	18	7	0	0	0	0
Reid, Dave, 1988–89 to 1989–90	LW	34, 14	147	18	40	58	31
Reynolds, Bobby, 1989–90	LW	20	7	1	1	2	0
Ribble, Pat, 1979–80	D	3	13	0	2	2	2
Richardson, Luke, 1987–88 to 1989–90	D	2	200	10	27	37	318
Robert, Rene, 1970–71; 1980–81 to 1981–82	RW	14	74	19	31	50	45
Robertson, Fred, 1931–32	D	17	8	0	0	0	23
Rodden, Edmund, 1927–28	F	12	25	3	6	9	36
Romnes, Doc, 1938–39	F	7	36	7	16	23	0
Root, Bill, 1984–85 to 1986–87	D	25	96	4	5	9	89
Rupp, Duane, 1964–65 to 1967–68	D	3, 4, 17	77	1	9	10	42
Sabourin, Bob, 1951–52	RW		1	0	0	0	2
Sabourin, Gary, 1974–75	RW	15	55	5	18	23	26
Saganiuk, Rocky, 1978–79 to 1982–83	RW	7, 8	230	56	62	118	164
Salming, Borje, 1973–74 to 1988–89	D	21	1099	148	620	768	1292
Samis, Phil, 1948 (playoffs); 1949–50	D	23	2	0	0	0	0
Sands, Charlie, 1932–33 to 1933–34	C	3, 16, 17	48	8	11	19	2
Schriner, Dave (Sweeney), 1939–40 to 1942–43; 1944–45 to 1945–46	LW	11	244	114	83	197	75
Schutt, Rod, 1985–86	LW	25	6	0	0	0	0
Scott, Ganton, 1926–27	RW		1	0	0	0	0
Secord, Al, 1987–88 to 1988–89	LW	20	114	20	37	57	292
Sedlbauer, Ron, 1980–81	LW	18	21	10	4	14	14
Seiling, Rod, 1962–63; 1974–75 to 1975–76	D	16	138	8	29	37	86
Selby, Brit, 1964–65 to 1966–67; 1968–69 to 1970–71	LW	8, 11, 15	169	29	30	59	93
Selwood, Brad, 1970–71 to 1971–72	D	3	100	6	27	33	71
Semenko, Dave	F	27	70	2	3	5	107
Shack, Eddie, 1960–61 to 1966–67; 1973–74 to 1974–75	RW	23	504	99	96	195	676
Shand, Dave, 1980–81; 1982–83	D	3, 4	48	0	5	5	62
Shannon, Darryl, 1988–89 to 1989–90	D	34	24	1	4	5	18
Shedden, Doug, 1988–89	RW	27	1	0	0	0	2
Shill, Jack, 1933–34; 1935–36 to 1936–37	LW	7, 19, 20, 18	42	4	6	10	26
Sittler, Darryl, 1970–71 to 1981–82	C	27	844	389	527	916	763
Sloan, Tod, 1947–48 to 1948–49; 1950–51 to 1957–58	C	11, 15, 20	549	162	184	346	650
Sly, Darryl, 1965–66; 1967–68	D	21	19	0	0	0	4
Smedsmo, Dale, 1972–73	LW	23	4	0	0	0	0
Smith, Art, 1927–28 to 1929–30	D	2, 3	101	13	6	19	188
Smith, Brad, 1985–86 to 1986–87	RW	29	89	10	24	34	258
Smith, Floyd, 1967–68 to 1969–70	RW	17	131	25	34	59	35
Smith, Sid, 1946–47 to 1957–58	LW	8, 16, 22, 24	601	186	183	369	94
Solinger, Bob, 1951–52 to 1954–55	LW	11, 21, 23, 25	99	10	11	21	19
Spencer, Brian, 1969–70 to 1971–72	LW	15, 22	95	10	20	30	192
Spring, Jesse, 1926–27	D		2	0	0	0	0
Stamler, Lorne, 1978–79	LW	12	45	4	3	7	2
Stanley, Allan, 1958–59 to 1967–68	D	26	633	47	186	233	318
Stanowski, Wally, 1939–40 to 1941–42; 1944–45 to 1947–48	D	2, 3, 20	282	20	74	94	106
Stastny, Marian, 1985–86	RW	10	70	23	30	53	21

All-Time Player Roster — *continued*

Name (Seasons Played)	Pos.	No.	GP	G	A	TP	PIM
Stemkowski, Pete, 1963–64 to 1967–68	C	12, 25	221	29	64	93	247
Stephenson, Bob, 79–80	RW	15	14	2	2	4	4
Stevens, Mike, 1989–90	LW	26	1	0	0	0	0
Stewart, Bill, 1983–84 to 1984–85	D	17	83	2	19	21	148
Stewart, Gaye, 1942–43; 1945–46 to 1947–48	LW	15, 16	165	81	52	133	52
Stewart, Ron, 1952–53 to 1964–65	RW	12, 19, 24	838	186	182	368	413
Stothers, Mike, 1987–88	D	25	18	0	1	1	42
Stoughton, Blaine, 1974–75 to 1975–76	LW	17	121	29	25	54	32
Strong, Ken, 1982–83 to 1984–85	LW	23	15	2	2	4	6
Sullivan, Frank, 1949–50; 1952–53	D	25	6	0	0	0	2
Sutherland, Bill, 1968–69	C	15	44	7	5	12	14
Sykes, Bob, 1974–75	LW		2	0	0	0	0
Taylor, Billy, 1939–40 to 1942–43; 1945–46	C	7, 19, 21	222	66	118	184	60
Taylor, Harry, 1946–47; 1948–49	C	17, 21	51	4	9	13	30
Terrion, Greg, 1982–83 to 1988–89	C	7	422	66	103	169	217
Thibaudeau, Gilles, 1989–90	C	7	21	7	11	18	13
Thomas, Cy, 1947–48	F	22	8	1	2	3	4
Thomas, Steve, 1984–85 to 1986–87	LW	12, 32	161	56	65	121	152
Thompson, Errol, 1970–71; 1972–73 to 1977–78	LW	12	365	126	119	245	70
Thoms, Bill, 1932–33 to 1938–39	C	7, 14, 16, 29	279	68	92	160	119
Thomson, Jim, 1945–46 to 1956–57	D	2, 20	717	15	208	223	830
Thomson, Rhys, 1942–43	D	17	18	0	2	2	22
Timgren, Ray, 1948–49 to 1952–53; 1954–55	LW	22	237	13	43	56	55
Trottier, Guy, 1970–71 to 1971–72	RW	11	113	28	17	45	37
Turnbull, Ian, 1973–74 to 1981–82	D	2	580	112	302	414	651
Ullman, Norm, 1967–68 to 1974–75	C	9	535	166	305	471	160
Unger, Garry, 1967–68	C	15	15	1	1	2	4
Vaive, Rick, 1979–80 to 1986–87	RW	22, 20	534	299	238	537	940
Valiquette, Jack, 1974–75 to 1977–78	C	8	172	33	66	99	52
Veitch, Darren, 1988–89	D	25	37	3	7	10	16
Verstraete, Leigh, 1982–83 to 1984–85; 1987–88	RW	34, 28	8	0	1	1	14
Voss, Carl, 1926–27; 1928–29	C		14	0	0	0	0
Walker, Kurt, 1975–76 to 1977–78	LW	26	71	4	5	9	152
Walton, Mike, 1965–66 to 1970–71	C	15, 16	257	84	109	193	184
Ward, Ron, 1969–70	C	25	18	0	1	1	2
Warner, Bob, 1976 (playoffs); 1976–77	D	16	10	1	1	2	4
Watson, Harry, 1946–47 to 1954–55	LW	4	500	163	122	285	111
Webster, Don, 1943–44	LW	19	27	7	6	13	28
Weir, Stan, 1975–76 to 1977–78	C	14	159	42	56	98	40
Wesley, Blake, 1985–86	D	28	27	0	1	1	21
Willard, Rod, 1982–83	LW	28	1	0	0	0	0
Williams, Dave (Tiger), 1974–75 to 1979–80	LW	22	407	109	132	241	1670
Wilson, John, 1959–60 to 1960–61	LW	19	73	15	17	32	8
Wilson, Ron, 1977–78 to 1979–80	RW	11, 14	64	7	15	22	6
Yaremchuk, Gary, 1981–82 to 1984–85	C	8	34	1	4	5	28
Yaremchuk, Ken, 1986–87 to 1988–89	C	16, 13, 34	47	6	13	19	28
Zanussi, Ron, 1980–81 to 1981–82	RW	39	55	3	8	11	20

All-Time Goaltending Roster

Name (Seasons Played)	No.	W	L	T	GPI	Min.	GA	GAA	SO
Bastien, Baz, 1945–46	1	0	4	1	5	300	20	4.00	0
Bell, Gord, 1945–46	1, 24	3	5	0	8	480	31	3.88	0
Bernhardt, Tim, 1984–85 to 1988–89	1	17	31	7	61	3,468	246	4.26	0
Bester, Allan, 1983–84 to 1989–90	30	69	85	16	199	11,016	723	3.94	7
Bibeault, Paul, 1943–44	1	13	14	2	29	1,740	87	3.00	5
Bower, Johnny, 1958–59 to 1969–70	1	220	161	79	472	27,396	1,145	2.51	32
Broda, Walter (Turk), 1936–37 to 1942–43; 1945–46 to 1951–52	1, 23	302	224	101	629	38,167	1,609	2.53	62
Chabot, Lorne, 1928–29 to 1932–33	1	108	72	34	214	13,024	477	2.20	33
Chadwick, Ed, 1955–56 to 1959–60	1, 20	57	89	34	180	10,740	529	2.96	14
Cheevers, Gerry, 1961–62	1	1	1	0	2	120	7	3.50	0
Crha, Jiri, 1979–80 to 1980–81	31	28	27	11	69	3,942	261	3.97	0
Dowie, Bruce, 1983–84	1	0	1	0	2	72	4	3.33	0
Edwards, Don, 1985–86	30	12	23	0	38	2,009	160	4.78	0
Edwards, Marv, 1969–70	31	10	9	4	25	1,420	77	3.25	1
Favell, Doug, 1973–74 to 1975–76	33	26	26	16	74	4,061	239	3.53	1
Gamble, Bruce, 1965–66 to 1970–71	1, 30	81	82	32	210	11,676	573	2.95	17
Grant, Ben, 1928–29 to 1931–32; 1943–44	1	13	17	4	37	2,190	135	3.70	3
Hainsworth, George, 1933–34 to 1936–37	1	79	48	20	147	9,157	345	2.26	19
Hamel, Pierre, 1974–75; 1978–79	31, 32, 1	1	2	0	5	196	18	5.51	0
Harrison, Paul, 1978–79 to 1979–80	30	17	29	5	55	2,895	192	3.98	1
Ironstone, Joe, 1927–28		1	0	0	1	70	0	0.00	1
Ing, Peter, 1989–90	31	0	2	1	3	182	18	5.93	0
Johnston, Ed, 1973–74	1	12	9	4	26	1,516	78	3.09	1
LaForest, Mark, 1989–90	1	9	14	0	27	1,343	80	3.89	0
Larocque, Michel, 1980–81 to 1982–83	1	16	35	13	74	3,942	315	4.80	0
Low, Ron, 1972–73	30	12	24	4	42	2,343	152	3.89	1
Lumley, Harry, 1952–53 to 1955–56	1	104	103	58	267	16,000	588	2.21	34
Maniago, Cesare, 1960–61	1	4	2	1	7	420	18	2.57	0
Marois, Jean, 1943–44		1	0	0	1	60	4	4.00	0
Mayer, Gil, 1949–50; 1953–54 to 1955–56	1, 22, 25	1	7	1	9	540	25	2.78	0
McCool, Frank, 1944–45 to 1945–46	1	34	31	7	72	4,320	242	3.36	4
McLachlan, Murray, 1970–71		0	1	0	2	25	4	9.60	0
McNamara, Gerry, 1960–61; 1969–70	1	2	2	1	7	323	15	2.79	0
McRae, Gord, 1972–73; 1974–75 to 1977–78	1, 31	21	32	10	71	3,799	221	3.49	1
Palmateer, Mike, 1976–77 to 1979–80; 1982–83 to 1983–84	29	129	112	41	296	16,868	964	3.43	15
Parent, Bernie, 1970–71 to 1971–72	30	24	25	12	65	3,755	162	2.59	4

All-Time Goaltending Roster — *continued*

Name (Seasons Played)	No.	W	L	T	GPI	Min.	GA	GAA	SO
Parent, Bob, 1981–82 to 1982–83	31	0	2	0	3	160	15	5.63	0
Plante, Jacques, 1970–71 to 1972–73	1	48	38	15	106	6,011	246	2.46	7
Reese, Jeff, 1987–88 to 1989–90	1, 35	12	14	5	36	1,836	138	4.51	0
Ridley, Curt, 1979–80 to 1980–81	1, 33	1	2	0	6	234	20	5.13	0
Roach, John Ross, 1926–27 to 1927–28	1	32	42	13	87	5,454	182	2.00	8
Rollins, Al, 1949–50 to 1951–52	23	57	30	24	112	6,663	228	2.05	11
Rutherford, Jim, 1980–81	1	4	10	2	18	961	82	5.12	0
Sawchuk, Terry, 1964–65 to 1966–67	30, 24	42	29	14	91	5,090	238	2.81	4
Simmons, Don, 1961–62 to 1963–64	1, 24	28	21	7	58	3,411	154	2.71	5
Smith, Al, 1965–66 to 1966–67; 1968–69	1, 30	4	3	1	10	457	23	3.02	0
Smith, Gary, 1965–66 to 1966–67	1	0	4	0	5	223	14	3.61	0
St. Croix, Rick, 1982–83 to 1984–85	1	11	28	2	47	2,467	191	4.65	0
Stein, Phil, 1939–40	1	0	0	1	1	70	2	1.71	0
Thomas, Wayne, 1975–76 to 1976–77	30, 33	38	37	18	97	5,487	312	3.41	3
Tremblay, Vincent, 1979–80 to 1982–83	1, 30	12	22	8	54	2,545	199	4.69	1
Wilson, Dunc, 1973–74 to 1974–75	1	17	22	7	49	2,805	154	3.29	1
Wilson, Ross (Lefty), 1955–56	1	0	0	0	1	13	0	0.00	0
Wregget, Ken, 1983–84 to 1988–89	31	55	112	17	200	10,923	791	4.34	2

John Ross Roach
HHF Archival Collection

All-Time Playoff Roster

Name	Pos.	GP	G	A	TP	PIM
Alexander, Claire	D	16	2	4	6	4
Allison, Mike	LW	13	3	5	8	15
Anderson, John	RW	17	3	7	10	0
Apps, Syl	C	69	25	28	53	16
Arbour, Al	D	9	0	0	0	8
Armstrong, George	RW	110	26	34	60	88
Armstrong, Murray	C	3	0	0	0	0
Ashby, Don	C	9	1	0	1	4
Aubin, Normand	C	1	0	0	0	0
Bailey, Irvine (Ace)	LW	21	3	4	7	12
Bailey, Bob	RW	6	0	2	2	4
Bailey, Reid	D	2	0	0	0	2
Balfour, Earl	LW	4	0	1	1	2
Barilko, Bill	D	47	5	7	12	104
Bathgate, Andy	RW	20	6	4	10	31
Baun, Bob	D	92	3	12	15	165
Benning, Jim	D	4	1	1	2	2
Bentley, Max	C	40	14	24	38	8
Blair, Andy	C	29	6	6	12	30
Blaisdell, Mike	RW	6	1	2	3	10
Bodnar, Gus	C	19	3	1	4	4
Boesch, Garth	D	34	2	5	7	18
Boivin, Leo	D	5	0	0	0	2
Boll, Frank (Buzz)	LW	28	7	3	10	13
Bolton, Hugh	D	17	0	5	5	14
Boothman, George	RW	5	2	1	3	2
Boschman, Laurie	C	6	1	1	2	25
Boudreau, Bruce	C	9	2	0	2	4
Boutette, Pat	RW	38	6	13	19	95
Boyer, Wally	C	4	0	1	1	0
Brewer, Carl	D	63	3	15	18	136
Brossart, Willie	D	1	0	0	0	0
Burrows, Dave	D	9	0	2	2	9
Butler, Jerry	RW	19	1	1	2	22
Cahan, Larry	D	4	0	0	0	0
Carlyle, Randy	D	16	0	2	2	28
Carr, Lorne	RW	37	6	7	13	11
Carriere, Larry	D	2	0	0	0	0
Chamberlain, Murph	C/LW	18	2	5	7	6
Chisholm, Lex	C	3	1	0	1	0
Church, Jack	D	16	1	1	2	14
Clancy, King	D	37	6	6	12	48
Clark, Wendel	LW	28	12	7	19	104
Conacher, Brian	LW	12	3	2	5	21
Conacher, Charlie	RW	41	14	12	26	43
Costello, Les	LW	6	2	2	4	2
Cotton, Harold	LW	34	2	7	9	35

All-Time Playoff Roster — *continued*

Name	Pos.	GP	G	A	TP	PIM
Courtnall, Russ	C	29	8	11	19	19
Cox, Dan	LW	4	0	1	1	4
Creighton, Dave	C	5	0	1	1	0
Cullen, Barry	RW	2	0	0	0	0
Cullen, Brian	C	19	3	0	3	2
Curran, Brian	D	11	0	1	1	60
Damphousse, Vincent	LW	23	1	8	9	20
Daoust, Dan	C	32	7	5	12	83
Darragh, Harold	F	7	0	1	1	2
Davidson, Bob	RW	82	5	17	22	79
Dawes, Bob	D	9	0	0	0	2
Day, Hap	D	45	4	7	11	54
DeGray, Dale	D	5	0	1	1	16
Derlago, Bill	C	10	4	0	4	8
Dickens, Ernie	D	13	0	0	0	4
Doraty, Ken	F	15	7	2	9	2
Dorey, Jim	D	10	0	2	2	40
Drillon, Gord	LW	45	22	13	35	10
Duff, Dick	LW	54	14	23	37	40
Duncan, Art	D	5	0	0	0	4
Dunn, Dave	D/F	10	1	1	2	41
Dupere, Denis	LW	14	0	0	0	0
Duris, Vitezslav	D	3	0	1	1	2
Ecclestone, Tim	LW	4	0	1	1	0
Edmundson, Garry	LW	9	0	1	1	4
Ehman, Gerry	RW	30	7	7	14	12
Ellis, Ron	RW	70	18	8	26	20
Erickson, Aut	D	1	0	0	0	2
Evans, Daryl	LW	1	0	0	0	0
Evans, Paul	C	2	0	0	0	0
Ezinicki, Bill	RW	34	4	7	11	69
Farrish, Dave	D	4	0	0	0	10
Fergus, Tom	C	20	9	12	21	14
Ferguson, George	C	42	8	9	17	25
Finnigan, Frank	RW	25	3	8	11	10
Flaman, Fernie	D	15	1	2	3	26
Flett, Bill	RW	5	0	0	0	2
Forsey, Jack	F	3	0	1	1	0
Fowler, Jim	D	18	0	3	3	2
Franceschetti, Lou	LW	5	0	1	1	26
Frycer, Miroslav	RW	17	3	8	11	16
Gardner, Cal	C	30	4	6	10	10
Gardner, Paul	C	6	0	1	1	4
Garland, Scott	C	7	1	2	3	35
Gavin, Stewart	LW	4	0	0	0	0
Gill, Todd	D	25	3	8	11	78
Gingras, Gaston	D	3	1	2	3	2
Glennie, Brian	D	32	0	1	1	66
Goldham, Bob	D	13	2	2	4	31
Goldup, Hank	LW	26	5	1	6	6
Gracie, Bob	LW	18	3	2	5	0
Gray, Alex	RW	4	0	0	0	0
Hamilton, Jack	C	11	2	1	3	0
Hamilton, Reg	D	60	6	5	11	52
Hammarstrom, Inge	LW	13	2	3	5	4
Hannan, Dave	RW	3	1	0	1	4
Hannigan, Gord	C	9	2	0	2	8
Harris, Billy	C	71	9	12	23	30
Harris, Billy	RW	4	0	1	1	2
Harrison, Jim	C	11	1	1	2	43
Henderson, Paul	LW	19	6	6	12	12
Heron, Bob (Red)	C	16	2	2	4	2

All-Time Playoff Roster — *continued*

Name	Pos.	GP	G	A	TP	PIM
Hickey, Pat	LW	5	0	0	0	2
Higgins, Paul	RW	1	0	0	0	0
Hill, Mel	RW	19	5	3	8	6
Hillman, Larry	D	32	2	3	5	8
Hollett, Flash	D	7	0	0	0	6
Horne, George	F	4	0	0	0	4
Horner, Red	D	71	7	10	17	166
Horton, Tim	D	97	9	32	41	135
Hurst, Ron	RW	3	0	2	2	4
Hutchison, Dave	D	6	0	3	3	23
Iafrate, Al	D	29	4	10	14	21
Ihnacak, Miroslav	LW	1	0	0	0	0
Ihnacak, Peter	C	28	4	10	14	25
Jackson, Art	C	16	0	3	3	2
Jackson, Harvey (Busher)	LW	54	17	8	25	41
James, Gerry	RW	15	1	0	1	8
Jarry, Pierre	LW	5	0	1	1	0
Jarvis, Wes	C	2	0	0	0	2
Jeffrey, Larry	LW	6	0	1	1	4
Johansen, Trevor	D	13	0	3	3	21
Johnson, Terry	D	5	0	0	0	10
Johnstone, Ross	D	3	0	0	0	0
Jones, Buck	D	6	0	0	0	8
Jones, Jim	C	19	1	5	6	11
Juzda, Bill	D	30	0	2	2	33
Kampman, Bingo	D	47	1	4	5	38
Kaszycki, Mike	C	2	0	0	0	2
Kehoe, Rick	RW	2	0	0	0	2
Kelly, Red	C	70	17	38	55	16
Kelly, Pep	F	39	7	6	13	10
Kennedy, Forbes	C	1	0	0	0	38
Kennedy, Ted	C	78	29	31	60	42
Keon, Dave	C	89	32	35	67	6
Kilrea, Hec	LW	11	2	0	2	6
Klukay, Joe	LW	56	11	9	20	14
Kordic, John	RW	5	0	1	1	33
Korn, Jim	D/LW	3	0	0	0	26
Kotsopoulos, Chris	D	17	1	0	1	28
Kurtenbach, Orland	C	4	0	0	0	20
Kurvers, Tom	D	5	0	3	3	4
Langelle, Pete	C	41	5	9	14	4
Lanz, Rick	D	14	1	3	4	29
Leeman, Gary	RW/D	24	7	14	21	34
Levinsky, Alex	D	23	1	0	1	20
Lewicki, Danny	LW	9	0	0	0	0
Ley, Rick	D	14	0	2	2	20
Litzenberger, Ed	RW	20	1	4	5	20
Lynn, Vic	LW	35	6	9	15	40
MacDonald, Parker	LW	4	0	0	0	4
MacKell, Fleming	C	27	5	8	13	22
MacMillan, Bill	RW	11	0	3	3	2
MacMillan, John	RW	8	0	0	0	0
Maguire, Kevin	RW	1	0	0	0	0
Mahovlich, Frank	LW	84	24	36	60	135
Maloney, Dan	LW	22	4	6	10	23
Mann, Norm	RW	1	0	0	0	0
Marcetta, Milan	C	3	0	0	0	0
Marker, Gus	RW	27	3	5	8	28
Marois, Daniel	RW	8	3	2	5	12
Marsh, Brad	D	5	1	0	1	2
Marshall, Don	LW	1	0	0	0	0
Martin, Terry	LW	10	2	0	2	16

All-Time Playoff Roster — *continued*

Name	Pos.	GP	G	A	TP	PIM
Maxwell, Brad	D	3	0	1	1	12
McCormack, John	C	6	1	0	1	0
McCreedy, John	RW	21	4	3	7	16
McDonald, Bucko	D	46	3	1	4	12
McDonald, Lanny	RW	45	20	17	37	22
McGill, Bob	D	12	0	0	0	35
McIntyre, John	C	2	0	0	0	2
McKechnie, Walt	C	6	4	3	7	9
McKenna, Sean	RW	2	0	0	0	0
McKenney, Don	C	18	4	8	12	0
McKenny, Jim	D	37	7	9	16	10
McLean, Jack	C	13	2	2	4	8
Meeker, Howie	RW	42	6	9	15	50
Melrose, Barry	D	7	0	2	2	38
Metz, Don	RW	47	7	8	15	10
Metz, Nick	LW	76	19	20	39	31
Mickey, Larry	RW	3	0	0	0	5
Migay, Rudy	C	15	1	0	1	20
Miller, Earl	F	7	0	0	0	0
Monahan, Garry	LW	15	2	1	3	9
Moore, Dick	RW	5	1	1	2	6
Morris, Moe	D	18	4	2	6	16
Morrison, Jim	D	16	0	1	1	12
Mortson, Gus	D	47	4	7	11	59
Mulhern, Richard	D	1	0	0	0	0
Neely, Bob	D	26	5	7	12	15
Nesterenko, Eric	RW	9	0	2	2	15
Nevin, Bob	RW	27	6	4	10	10
Nigro, Frank	C	3	0	0	0	2
Nylund, Gary	D	10	0	2	2	25
Olczyk, Ed	C	11	6	6	12	16
Oliver, Murray	C	4	1	2	3	0
Olmstead, Bert	LW	29	8	9	17	23
O'Neill, Tom (Windy)	RW	4	0	0	0	6
Osborne, Mark	LW	20	4	9	13	34
Paiement, Wilf	RW	6	0	2	2	19
Pappin, Jim	RW	13	7	8	15	12
Parsons, George	LW	7	3	2	5	11
Pearson, Scott	LW	2	2	0	2	10
Pelyk, Mike	D	40	0	3	3	41
Pettinger, Eric	LW	4	1	0	1	8
Pilote, Pierre	D	4	0	1	1	4
Poddubny, Walt	LW	13	7	2	9	4
Poile, Bud	C	13	4	4	8	6
Pratt, Tracy	D	4	0	0	0	0
Pratt, Walter (Babe)	D	24	3	9	12	20
Price, Noel	D	5	0	0	0	2
Primeau, Joe	C	38	5	18	23	12
Pronovost, Marcel	D	16	1	0	1	14
Pulford, Bob	C	89	25	26	51	126
Quenneville, Joel	D	6	0	1	1	4
Quinn, Pat	D	4	0	0	0	13
Ramage, Rob	D	5	1	2	3	20
Reaume, Marc	D	19	0	2	2	8
Regan, Larry	RW	22	4	4	8	2
Reid, Dave	LW	3	0	0	0	0
Richardson, Luke	D	7	0	0	0	22
Robert, Rene	RW	3	0	2	2	2
Robertson, Fred	D	7	0	0	0	0
Romnes, Doc	F	10	1	4	5	0
Root, Bill	D	20	1	2	3	25

All-Time Playoff Roster — *continued*

Name	Pos.	GP	G	A	TP	PIM
Saganiuk, Rocky	RW	6	1	0	1	15
Salming, Borje	D	81	12	37	49	91
Samis, Phil	D	5	0	1	1	2
Sands, Charlie	C	13	3	2	5	2
Schriner, Dave (Sweeney)	LW	47	14	10	24	22
Secord, Al	LW	6	1	0	1	16
Sedlbauer, Ron	LW	2	0	1	1	2
Seiling, Rod	D	17	0	1	1	6
Selby, Brit	LW	8	0	0	0	4
Selwood, Brad	D	5	0	0	0	4
Shack, Eddie	RW	57	6	3	9	107
Shand, Dave	D	7	1	0	1	13
Shill, Jack	LW	13	0	3	3	8
Sittler, Darryl	C	64	25	40	65	120
Sloan, Tod	C	26	5	6	11	59
Smith, Art	D	4	1	1	2	8
Smith, Brad	RW	17	3	2	5	44
Smith, Floyd	RW	4	0	0	0	0
Smith, Sid	LW	44	17	10	27	2
Spencer, Brian	LW	6	0	1	1	17
Stanley, Allan	D	82	4	27	31	60
Stanowski, Wally	D	60	3	14	17	13
Stastny, Marian	RW	3	0	0	0	0
Stemkowski, Pete	C	22	5	10	15	53
Stewart, Gaye	LW	18	2	7	9	8
Stewart, Ron	RW	82	10	18	28	56
Stoughton, Blaine	LW	7	4	2	6	2
Taylor, Billy	C	28	5	13	18	9
Taylor, Harry	C	1	0	0	0	0
Terrion, Greg	C	32	1	9	10	37
Thomas, Steve	LW	23	8	11	19	22
Thompson, Errol	LW	27	5	4	9	9
Thoms, Bill	C	39	6	9	15	4
Thomson, Jim	D	63	2	13	15	135
Timgren, Ray	LW	30	3	9	12	6
Trottier, Guy	RW	9	1	0	1	16
Turnbull, Ian	D	55	13	32	45	94
Ullman, Norm	C	26	3	6	9	6
Vaive, Rick	RW	32	14	9	23	53
Valiquette, Jack	C	23	3	6	9	4
Walker, Kurt	LW	16	0	0	0	34
Walton, Mike	C	16	4	3	7	6
Warner, Bob	D	4	0	0	0	0
Watson, Harry	LW	50	14	9	23	27
Webster, Don	LW	5	0	0	0	12
Weir, Stan	C	29	6	5	11	0
Williams, Dave (Tiger)	LW	44	5	11	16	240
Wilson, John	LW	10	1	2	3	2
Wilson, Ron	RW	6	1	3	4	2
Yaremchuk, Ken	C	12	0	2	2	10
Zanussi, Ron	RW	3	0	0	0	0

Player Profiles

Syl Apps 47
(Photo) Imperial Oil Turofsky Collection, HHF

George Armstrong 72
(Photo) HHF Archival Collection

Ace Bailey 25
(Photo) Imperial Oil Turofsky Collection, HHF

Bill Barilko 78
(Photo) Imperial Oil Turofsky Collection, HHF

Bobby Baun 103
(Photo) HHF Archival Collection

Johnny Bower 92
(Photo) Imperial Oil Turofsky Collection, HHF

Turk Broda 80
(Photo) HHF Archival Collection

Lorne Chabot 27
(Photo) Imperial Oil Turofsky Collection, HHF

King Clancy 35
(Photo) Bill Stewart Collection, HHF

Wendel Clark 132
(Photo) NHL Publications, HHF

Charlie Conacher 33
(Photo) Montreal Forum

Hap Day 23
(Photo) HHF Archival Collection

Gordie Drillon 45
(Photo) Tom Gaston Collection, HHF

Babe Dye 19
(Photo) HHF Archival Collection

Red Horner 32
(Photo) HHF Archival Collection

Tim Horton 110
(Photo) Imperial Oil Turofsky Collection, HHF

Al Iafrate 138
(Photo) Bruce Bennett Studios

Teeder Kennedy 55
(Photo) Imperial Oil Turofsky Collection, HHF

Dave Keon 91
(Photo) HHF Archival Collection

Gary Leeman 134
(Photo) Bruce Bennett Studios

Frank Mahovlich 89
(Photo) Imperial Oil Turofsky Collection, HHF

Frank McCool 56
(Photo) HHF Archival Collection

Lanny McDonald 125
(Photo) HHF Archival Collection

Mike Palmateer 127
(Photo) Bruce Bennett Studios

Babe Pratt 65
(Photo) Imperial Oil Turofsky Collection, HHF

John Ross Roach 20
(Photo) HHF Archival Collection

Borje Salming 119
(Photo) Miles S. Nadal Collection, HHF

Darryl Sittler 122
(Photo) Bruce Bennett Studios

Rick Vaive 131
(Photo) Miles S. Nadal Collection, HHF